With Me

A CAPTIVATING JOURNEY INTO INTIMACY

Ben R. Peters

With Me

A CAPTIVATING JOURNEY INTO INTIMACY

ISBN: 0-9767685-5-0

Open Heart Ministries
15648 Bombay Blvd.
S. Beloit, IL 61080
www.ohmint.org
benrpeters@juno.com

Contents

Preface

"THE LORD IS MY SHEPHERD, I SHALL NOT WANT." How many books have been written and how many songs have been sung about Psalm 23? How many sermons have been preached from that text and how many friends and family members have been laid to rest with the reading of those classic words? Of course, we could never answer the above questions. Psalm 23 has undoubtedly been the best loved and most quoted chapter of Scripture, including both the Old and the New Testaments.

As one who has grown up in the church and ministered the gospel for several decades, I have personally heard and used this Psalm hundreds of times, but until recently I had never seen what seems so obvious to me today.

I had always seen the Psalm like the vast majority of Bible teachers and students. It was a beautiful Hebrew poem or song about all the wonderful things the Good Shepherd does for His His sheep. His blessings include provision for life, protection in danger and blessings of His favor. This perspective on the psalm does give us some understanding of our shepherd, but there is so much more to learn from this psalm when you see it from a whole new perspective.

That new perspective is simply this: Psalm 23 describes your journey and mine. It clearly outlines our pilgrimage from our initial salvation experience to our eternal reward. When you see the psalm from this perspective, it will open your eyes to incredible treasures of truth. Please join me on this journey as we go prospecting for precious gems in this choice Old Testament chapter.

The insights and treasures discovered in this adventure will apply to us as individuals in the family of God, but it will also provide some special insights for leaders who want to be as much like the Great Shepherd as possible. The order of events in Psalm 23 is very significant, and those with the calling of pastor should be especially encouraged with the wisdom God has released through this classic Hebrew psalm.

Chapter One

Who Needs a Shepherd Anyway?

A LESSON FROM JAMES

The little lamb was not so little any more. In fact, James was feeling quite grown up. He was quite sure that he was completely capable of taking care of himself. He really didn't like all the rules that were being imposed on him. He knew that there was greener grass just on the other side of some trees and bushes. Some of his young friends had already snuck away to check it out and were boasting about it to him. James was getting very tired of his parents telling him to obey the shepherd. Late one night as he lay down to go to sleep, after being told to do so by his mother, James decided to join the other young and adventurous sheep the very next time they went to the forbidden pasture.

James was quite excited about his decision. He couldn't wait to get out from under the constant surveillance of his family members and the shepherd, who seemed so strict and overly cautious to him. He thought to himself, "Who needs a shepherd anyway?

Maybe the little lambs and the weak old sheep do, but not me. I can take care of myself, just fine."

The time came when James and his friends noticed that the shepherd was busy with a wounded sheep. They ran as fast as their wooly legs could carry them and headed for the little pathway into the cluster of brush and trees. As soon as they were out of sight of the shepherd, they all breathed a sigh of relief. As far as they could tell, none of the other sheep had noticed them slip away.

It took only a few minutes to get to the pasture on the other side. The grass was fresh and greener than any grass James had ever seen. The other young sheep had been here a couple of times before and started munching right away. They weren't worried about anything and felt so free, away from the watchful eyes of the older sheep and the shepherd. James never even noticed that across the narrow pasture was an even thicker wooded area, which was full of beautiful fresh spring foliage.

When they had eaten their fill, they waddled over to a small creek that flowed through the forbidden pasture and had a wonderful drink. The water seemed so much clearer than the little pond where they normally drank. After they had drunk as much as their young bellies could hold, they slipped back to the pasture where the rest of the sheep had been grazing on the inferior grass. James noticed how poor the grass looked compared to where he had just been. The flock had been there for some time and the grass had been trampled on repeatedly.

James concluded that the shepherd didn't really have their best interest at heart. Why would he make them stay in the old pasture when there was such good grass just a few minutes away? He just seemed so unaware that young and energetic sheep could use a little excitement and adventure. Why should they have to stick with all the babies and the old and weaker sheep? The shepherd was always so concerned about keeping them safe that they couldn't have much fun without getting into trouble. James was already looking forward to his next adventure as he slipped back into the flock, trying to make it look like he had been there all the time.

No one seemed to notice that he had been gone, and he felt relieved. This was surely the life he wanted to live. He was already thinking of excuses to tell his family members if he was missed. "Oh, I was with some of the other younger sheep on the other side of the pasture." Or better yet, "I had to check up on one of my friends. I heard he was sick, so I went to visit him." That should take the pressure off him if his parents started to notice he was gone.

It wasn't long until the next illicit adventure took place. Again, it went off without a hitch. It was a lot of fun to just hang out with the other young sheep and sneak off whenever all the other older sheep were grazing with their heads down. They enjoyed telling each other stories about how old-fashioned their parents were.

About the fifth time they snuck off to the greener pasture, they had just begun to gorge themselves on the lush green grass when something began to move out of the woods into the tall vegetation. Keeping as low as possible, a pack of hungry wolves began to encircle the little group of rebels. They knew exactly what to do to get some fresh meat to feed their growing cubs. When the tightening circle was almost complete, James just happened to lift his head. He had heard about wolves, but thought of them pretty much as a fairy tale. He had never seen one in real life, but now he was looking at several of them.

James let out a terrified, "Baa, Baa!" All his buddies froze momentarily at the sound of his voice, knowing something was terribly wrong. In a split second, they could all see one or more of the hungry predators. As quickly as they could, they fled towards the pathway that headed home to the safety of the shepherd and the flock. But of course, with their overburdened bellies, they were no match for the fleet pack of ravenously hungry wolves. Before they had moved ten feet, James and all of his buddies were being knocked to the ground by one or more of the wolves.

James felt totally helpless to defend himself. The wolf's teeth penetrated through the layer of wool into his neck. The pain was excruciating. How he wished he had stayed with the flock. The other young rebel sheep were bleating in terror as they also felt the sting of the teeth of hungry wolves.

Suddenly, when terror had turned into despair and hopelessness, they all heard a familiar voice. It was stronger and louder than James had ever heard it before. It was the shepherd. He had his long staff in his hand and swung it with incredible force, landing a direct blow on the back of the wolf attacking James. The surprised wolf let out a blood-curdling howl and ran as fast as he could towards the woods, obviously injured by the powerful blow of the shepherd's staff.

The other wolves immediately left their prey and fled quickly back to the protection of their woods. The shepherd shouted loudly at them, warning them to never come back to touch his sheep. Then he turned his attention to the wounded young sheep who had been feeding in the forbidden pasture.

All of the young sheep were hurting pretty badly. One of them, James' closest friend, and the leader of the group, was in rather critical condition having lost a lot of blood. The shepherd quickly did what he could to stop the bleeding and carried him in his arms, while the other wounded sheep, including James, limped home in pain and shame behind their shepherd, who had become their savior.

James had a lot of explaining to do, but his parents were pretty understanding and so thankful that the shepherd had saved his life. In the hours of quiet time, recovering from his injuries, James decided that he did need a shepherd after all. Whenever the shepherd came around to check on him and treat his wounds, James would look at him with a whole new respect and a deep, heart-felt love. His days of being his own boss had gone forever. He decided to make a strong commitment to this wonderful shepherd as long as he lived.

Within a few days, the wise shepherd led the whole flock to another pasture a ways up a nearby hillside. James couldn't believe what he saw, when they finally arrived. This new pasture was even better than the forbidden pasture where he had grazed with his adventurous friends. The grass was even taller and greener and the quiet creek was colder and purer than the other as well. The shepherd had been waiting for the right timing, knowing when the lambs would be strong enough for the journey, and when the climate was just right at the higher altitude.

James' love and respect for his shepherd grew every day. What he noticed though, that he still had a hard time believing, was that his shepherd seemed to be really fond of him and actually enjoyed spending time with him. The shepherd seems so different than before, but James knew that the shepherd hadn't changed. It had to be him that had changed. The shepherd seemed so affectionate now, but James guessed correctly that the difference was that he used to hide from the shepherd, while now he looked forward to seeing him every day.

Soon James was feeling like new again and with his parents' permission, he began to spend more time with the shepherd. Like a big fluffy puppy dog, he followed his master wherever he went. The shepherd always spoke lovingly to him and taught him much about the art of being a shepherd.

It wasn't long until James was fully grown and a very handsome young ram. The shepherd had taught him well, and now was making him a guard sheep to help keep an eye on the younger sheep and the little lambs. James felt so honored, and he determined to be faithful and protect the younger sheep from the dangers that he knew about so well. The shepherd was trusting in him and he would never let him down again.

James felt very good about his new life. Instead of fearing and despising his shepherd, he was now his very best friend. He felt so secure and safe, so honored and blessed. His shepherd had exalted him among the other sheep, even though he had rebelled against his authority. Of course, James didn't know what the word "grace" meant, but he had learned that his shepherd was pretty awesome, so forgiving and so very kind. His love for him deepened every day, and he would never forget the day that he learned how much he needed his wonderful shepherd.

ALL WE LIKE SHEEP HAVE GONE ASTRAY

The story of James is our story. Until we realize we need a Shepherd, we cannot be blessed with the benefits of a life of walking with Him.

Psalm 23 begins with the simple statement: "The Lord is my Shepherd." Just as James didn't think he needed a shepherd, so many of us came to that conclusion at some point in our lives. But somewhere on the timeline of our life, we found ourselves in trouble. We found out that the bright lights of "Sin Street" were an illusion. We found that the "substances" that gave us our "highs" had hooks in them. We bit the bait, but found out that we had swallowed the hook, line and sinker.

We were being attacked by the hungry wolves, who wanted to totally devour us. Somehow, we knew who could help us when we were desperate enough. We shouted out a loud "Baa, Baa, Jesus help me." Maybe He used someone led by the Holy Spirit, who spoke to us about God's grace, just when we were at the end of our rope. However it happened, we knew we needed a Shepherd and confessed to being a needy sheep.

In my case, I simply understood, as a four-year-old, that I needed Jesus in my heart if I wanted to go to Heaven and escape the place of fire and torment called hell. As a child, I knew I needed help. Most little ones understand that. As Heidi Baker says, "The children get it!" It's when we start thinking we are pretty smart or powerful that we get into trouble and reject the loving guidance of the Great Shepherd.

When we did come to our senses, we realized that we weren't quite as smart as we thought we were. In fact, we had come close to being a total idiot, when we think about the logic we employed in our justification of our wild, unbridled behavior.

Basically, we become the most intelligent and wise when we come to the conclusion that we cannot control our destiny, and we are not the brightest star in the universe. Rather, we are blessed to have that Someone who actually cares about us for some reason. He is willing to watch over us and guide us and give us His protection. He has already made the ultimate sacrifice to prove His love to us. Let's just love Him and serve Him now because He first loved and served us.

I SHALL NOT WANT

When we came to Jesus, we may have tried everything else first. We may have felt very strong and independent, only to find our strength failing us in the time of crisis. **We found ourselves in want.**

When we met Jesus, we were overwhelmed with His love and compassion. We got a glimpse of His power and glory and for the first time in a long time, we felt secure. We now had Someone who really cared, Someone who would always be there and Someone who was so strong that He could do anything He wanted. We could say with confidence and joy, "I shall not want" or in other words, "I am safe, I am secure and everything I need is going to be provided."

Let's sum up the first chapter. When we finally admit that we need a shepherd and cry out for help, Jesus comes to us, saves or rescues us and makes us feel totally secure. This is a totally wonderful feeling after being so insecure and helpless, while trying hard to be our own shepherd.

Chapter Two

Gourmet Grass and Sparkling Water

After we submit our lives to the care of the Good Shepherd, we are usually treated to some wonderful and delightful delicacies. At the beginning of our journey, it seems that miracles and answers to prayer are coming every day. We get very excited and zealous, telling anyone who will listen how awesome our Shepherd is.

It's like being a baby and having everything done for you. A baby gets to eat without ever working. It is loved and cared for even when it makes messes several times a day and leaves them for someone else to clean up. No matter what it does, a baby is loved and delighted in. We, as parents, see ourselves in our children and have vision for who they will become. God likewise delights in us as baby Christians. He sees Himself in us and looks forward to us fulfilling our destiny and purpose through His power. The following statement is not totally true, but I've heard it said that "Baby Christians get all their prayers answered."

Starting the Christian life, we need lots of nourishment to get us off on the right foot. God wants us to be strong in Him and full of His power. Paul declares: "As newborn babies, desire the pure milk of the word, that you may grow thereby." (I Peter 2:2) We are very blessed to have the Word of God so available to us in the western world. We need to encourage our babies to eat and drink from the fountain of His Word.

HE MAKES ME LIE DOWN IN GREEN PASTURES

What does the green pasture represent? First of all, the verse declares that our Great Shepherd causes us to lie down in the green grass. As we know, sheep lie down after they have grazed for some time to chew their cud until it has been properly processed. Lying down indicates we have been feeding in a peaceful setting and now are able to rest without fear while we process what we have taken in.

The grass, which contains the nutrition every sheep needs, represents the written Word of God. His word is our "bread." We grow strong when we take His word into our spirit and soul.

I had been a Christian for fourteen years when I began Bible College/Seminary, but I had an encounter with God my freshman year that made it like I was starting over in my Christian walk. It was a new beginning and it was like I was a baby again, with an insatiable hunger for the Word. Every morning I would spend an hour or two reading, praying and weeping over the Bible as I read about the power of the early church.

The Living Word became my bread and often my breakfast. I was receiving such nourishment from the Bible that I didn't want to sacrifice the green pastures I was feeding in to take the time to eat the natural cafeteria food. This daily feasting gave me incredible strength in my inner man. I found more than enough strength to resist the temptations which had formerly conquered me. I also discovered a strength in my character that enabled me to love those who attacked me.

Even as a child, because of parents who totally believed in the Bible as God's Living Word, I was encouraged to read and memorize it. I was even paid for memorization. The first year it was a penny per verse. That won't cut it today, but in those days it was worth it for a little boy with nothing better to do. Every year I got a penny raise until, at four cents per verse, my parents couldn't afford to raise it to five cents. Actually, this was my main source of income for some time, until I became a teenager and started working in our printing shop and in the sugar beet fields of southern Alberta, Canada.

I also enjoyed reading the Bible, partly for bragging rights at Sunday School, DVBS, boys clubs, camps and church. I read every word, so I could be totally honest when I said I had read the whole Bible. I finished my third reading by the time I was ten years old, if my memory serves me correctly. While my motives were not completely pure or mature, God was nurturing my character with the knowledge of His Word. That knowledge became a foundation for future insights and revelation for the teaching ministry I have today.

Now I find times when Scriptures come to mind when the Holy Spirit wants to speak to me. Not long ago, on a journey from Chicago to Washington State, I had risen very early in order to cover a lot of miles in the motor home and get to our destination as soon as possible. I had neglected to read my Bible before I got started, and I was wishing I could just open the Bible for a few minutes to get something to chew on while I was driving.

Suddenly I realized a Bible verse had just crossed my mind for no reason. It was the middle of May and the verse was from Luke 2, a Christmas passage. I thought to myself, "Where did that verse come from?"

Because I had grazed for years on the Word of God, I was able to lie down and chew the cud. In the next hour or so, the Holy Spirit gave me several wonderful insights to compare those days with today. In the weeks following, I shared these insights in at least a half a dozen churches, and at a large pastors' conference as part of the message God was giving me for them.

The insights gained from the above revelation, along with a second similar experience, are shared in the last chapter of this book written as a bonus, specifically for pastors. If you are not a pastor and read it anyway, you may get away with it, but don't be surprised if God doesn't call you to become a pastor—just to punish you. Of course, I'm only kidding!

HE LEADS ME BESIDE THE STILL WATERS

Water often is symbolic of the Holy Spirit. Water not only refreshes and oxygenates our bodies, but being a liquid and not a solid, it can move and flow from place to place. Jesus leads us as young Christians to the life and freedom of flowing with the Holy Spirit. While the green grass can represent the written Word, the Logos, the still waters can represent the voice of the Holy Spirit, the *Rhema* Word of God.

Unfortunately, many young Christian converts are not introduced to the work and ministry of the Holy Spirit. His ministry is minimized and the young lambs who need the clear water flowing through them are denied His fullness. They often can't fulfill the demands of a Christian walk without His power and give up, feeling like failures.

Others, with strong will power and determination, keep the letter of the Logos, but become somewhat rigid and critical of others who don't have the will power to live by the rules given to them. They may develop great habits and disciplines, but they become too much like the Pharisees to accomplish a lot for the Lord.

As sheep of the Great Shepherd, we need both the green pastures and the quiet waters. We must be people both of the Word and of the Spirit. God wants to join the two into one. We can't walk on one leg, and we can't live the Christian life without the Word or the Spirit.

The gift of the word of knowledge, mentioned in I Corinthians 12, is a great example of how the Holy Spirit helps people grow in their early walk with their Shepherd. I will never forget one night in Argentina, when my mentor, Elmer. R. Burnette, called up several ladies and gave them detailed information about what was happening in their lives. One was told she was sitting on a green couch in her living room, weeping because her husband was unsaved. He assured her that God had heard her prayers. The next night her husband came and got saved. The words of knowledge did much to build the faith of those called up, and it also built the faith of the whole crowd who had come to see what was happening.

On two separate occasions, Elmer ministered to pastors and leaders with clear and powerful prophetic visions and words of knowledge. The missionary, who knew the pastors well, verified every word as being clearly from God. The pastors invariably wept like babies as God revealed His love and concern for them, through the fact that He was depicting their journey, via the visions given to Elmer.

These pastors and leaders grew in their own faith and ministry. Five new churches were started and the spiritual growth of the other churches was very strong. It all had to do with the flowing of the Water of Life, which ministered to their spirits.

Pastor Burnette also ministered to me with a prophetic vision the Lord gave him. I have detailed this in previous books, but the clincher was that he could identify a person he had never met as my aunt, after seeing her in the vision and then in a photo album. Later he met her and told her that when he had seen her in the vision, her hair was longer. She commented that she had just had her hair cut.

This experience, along with hundreds of miracles and about one thousand conversions, impacted me in a powerful way. I came home with a passion and a zeal to flow in the power of the Holy Spirit. My ministry changed radically from those six incredible weeks, reviving the fire of my passion from my earlier days as a freshman in Bible College. I am very grateful to God for both the green pastures and the clear flowing waters. I was very blessed to have been introduced early in my life to both of these awesome sources of spiritual nutrition.

Chapter Three

Restoration is Preparation

HE RESTORES MY SOUL

As we illustrated earlier, sheep often come to the conclusion that they need a shepherd when they are going through a crisis or emergency. Of course, before the straw that broke the camel's back (the ultimate crisis that brought them to Jesus), they had been through a lot of previous pain and suffering. Because of this, many of them come into the fold with a multitude of serious injuries in the soul realm.

James, the young sheep, needed his wounds attended to, but how much more do human hearts and souls need a healing touch from Jesus after being torn to shreds in their inner man by the vicious enemy of God? The wolves, who frequently come disguised in sheep's clothing can be brutal. People, both believers and unbelievers, can be used by our enemy without knowing what they are doing. Even completely well-meaning Christians have inflicted serious wounds on non-Christians and weak Christians alike.

Pastors must take time to bring healing to the young converts, because if they don't, those converts are not going to be successful in the next phase of their Christian life. Here is where we as Christian leaders go wrong so many times in trying to raise up godly young Christians.

In the following chapter we will be dealing with "paths of righteousness," which speaks about discipleship. If we don't bring healing to the souls of the young sheep, we will find that we are having great difficulty leading them in these paths of righteousness. Without a healthy understanding of God's love and forgiveness, they can't make it down that path. They need a time for recovery and healing.

As leaders, we can't just assume that because new converts are excited about what Jesus has done, that they are therefore ready to be leaders and walk in righteousness and spiritual character, etc. We should rather assume that very soon they will be confronted with situations that will try to take them out early. They will have some character flaws and unpredictable reactions to other people, based on the fact that they have been seriously wounded and people are touching an open sore in their heart.

We won't be able to address and totally heal every individual hurt and wound in every young convert's life, but we ought to take time to deal with as many of the major ones as possible in the early stages of the new believer's Christian walk. The less baggage they bring with them on the road, the less they will have to weigh them down and take them out.

Before we deal with some of the most common wounds, let's explain what we mean when we use the term "pastor." Our common usage of the word refers to the administrative and speaking leader of the local church. To be more biblical, I would rather look at the gifting/calling of the leader before I call him or her a "pastor." Most local church leaders are actually apostles, prophets, evangelists or teachers. A few are true pastors, (usually with small churches) but many are gifted more in apostolic administration, prophetic proclamation, evangelistic outreach or revelatory teaching.

The true pastor is one who focuses on the individual sheep and his or her spiritual health. Pastors are not usually the most visionary or scholarly, etc. They simply love and care for people and want to bring healing and happiness to them. They are often the people in the pews. They may be leading home groups or showing hospitality, visiting hospitals, jails and nursing homes. They are care-givers and lovers of people.

There should be many of these in every local church and they should be assigned to the new converts along with those who teach well the foundation truths of the Word of God. Pastors and teachers prepare the sheep for the inevitable journey which always follows the green pastures and clear waters.

One further note: Unlike the Hebrew and Greek and all other languages that I know about, we have two separate words in English for the same thing. The word pastor is really the same word as shepherd. There is no distinction in the original text. In Acts 20 and in I Peter 5, elders were told to "Shepherd the flock of God." The word used is the verb form of the noun translated "pastors" in Ephesians 4:11. That passage lists the five ministries which God gave to the church.

Bitterness and Unforgiveness

Probably the biggest problem in the soul of man is bitterness and unforgiveness. So many ministries have been called to minister to this need of man that it is not really necessary to go into detail about this subject here. But let's be clear. This issue takes out or immobilizes untold millions of saints from every culture and background worldwide.

The true pastor should deal with this issue thoroughly in every new convert. Jesus totally connected receiving forgiveness to giving forgiveness in the prayer He taught His disciples to pray. I've seldom heard a prayer for salvation that included forgiving others, but it seems that it really should be an integral part of every salvation prayer. The new converts should, of course, be led into a more detailed discussion of this important subject, but it would be wise to include it in the salvation prayer right at the start of their spiritual walk.

The consequences of unforgiveness or bitterness are not only related to eternal destiny, but also to spiritual paralysis in this life. Like a tumor which robs the body of nutrition and energy, unforgiveness and bitterness siphon off the spiritual strength that God wants every child of His to experience daily. Shepherds need to encourage new believers to deal with this issue immediately, while the heart is still tender.

Guilt, Condemnation and Shame

This three-headed monster will never give up trying to destroy the new Christian. It will be always waiting, always lurking in the shadows, watching for the opportune moment to strike at its victim. Pastors should always be aware that this monster is an enemy that must be recognized and destroyed by the Sword of the Spirit. Let the teachers proclaim what Jesus did to this monster/dragon on the cross. See that the convert accepts the teaching, not

RESTORATION IS PREPARATION

only with the mind, but in the heart.

Guilt is the first level of pain in the soul when we have violated God and His laws, which includes loving our neighbor as ourselves. Guilt is a frequent companion on life's journey, but if we learn to recognize it and quickly repent, we can wave goodbye to it after a very brief encounter.

Condemnation is guilt taken to the level of despair and hopelessness. It results from guilt that is not dealt with through the truths of the Word of God. Guilt tells us that we have done wrong and with it comes fear that we will be caught and punished. Condemnation tells us that we have already been caught and tried and sentenced. With condemnation there is no hope of being found "not guilty." Rather, we have already been given a life sentence without hope of parole.

When people walk in condemnation, they have great difficulty walking the straight and narrow. There is often an attitude of, "Why try?" Many are walking the Christian Highway of Life not believing there is any hope for them. They are just trying to stay out of more trouble and hoping no one will notice how messed up they are.

Shame is a dark prison of the soul that we try to keep out of our conscious world, but it never really goes away. We may try to act like everything is fine, but the inner pain in the soul is always there. Accompanying shame is a numbing fear that people will find out what we have done. If people already know about it there is that "bowed down" posture that keeps us from looking up to the One Who gives us the Light of His Glory. Shame tries to stay in the shadows. It fears being put on stage for obvious reasons.

Sexual issues are probably the leading sources of shame in

our lives. I'm sure almost every Christian has had to deal with this aspect of shame and I am no exception. Even when we are raised in God-fearing homes, flesh is there and temptations often find us weak and vulnerable. Accepting forgiveness and healing is so essential, and it is so important that we address these issues in new converts, as well as those who have been Christians, but never have had anyone to open their heart up to.

God has given us clear and precious promises to defeat this three-headed monster. No new convert should spend any significant time as a Christian walking with guilt, condemnation and shame. As shepherds, we need to restore and heal the soul of every Christian to prepare them for their adventure with destiny.

Abandonment and Orphan Spirit

Many, who are discovering that they need a Shepherd after all, have made that discovery after being abandoned by those they trusted for security and love. They come with a feeling of worthlessness or with an orphan spirit. These are extremely deep wounds that don't heal overnight.

After all, why would someone totally abandon me when they were all I had? If I am worthy of love, why would they desert me and leave me as an orphan. No matter how much these people are told they are special, their mind says, "If that were true, that special person in my life would not have dumped me like a load of garbage."

Of course most young people go through this to some extent when they date and break up, but for many children, and even adults, what they experience is incredibly painful. Unmarried parents gave them up for adoption, or their parents divorced or separated and blamed their children. Even if they didn't speak the blame, the children feel the blame because they somehow feel they should have been able to stop it and they failed.

New converts (along with many older Christians) need to be made to understand the "Spirit of Adoption" that sees us all as being orphans until we are adopted into the "Family of God." They also need to feel the love and acceptance from loving shepherds that have patience to prove that love, even when it is resisted because of the persistent pain in the heart of the one who was abandoned.

Many Christians also have an "orphan spirit" from being spiritually abandoned by spiritual leaders. When church leaders leave their churches for a better position or because of opposition, etc., there are often deep spiritual wounds in those who looked up to them as spiritual "fathers." Some of these leaders have fallen into immorality and others into cultish manipulation, etc. It is very difficult for many of their followers to ever trust another spiritual leader, and they live with that feeling of being a spiritual orphan. Pastors need to find the grace and wisdom to understand and bring restoration to the souls of these wounded sheep.

Fear, Self-Pity, Anger, Lust, Jealousy, Chemical Dependency, etc.

There are so many different fleshly vices that can darken and pollute the soul. The sub-title above lists only a few of them, but every single one of them can be deadly and a major stumbling-block on the pathway of righteousness and discipleship. Each one of them can become a habit or pattern that has us programmed to react in a negative way to any unexpected circumstance.

All of these vices are designed by our enemy to keep us from fulfilling our destiny. Each one is deceptive. Each one is a cruel and unusual punishment for the soul. Help from Heaven is needed and is available to those who cry out to Jesus. Pastors must take time to open every heart to allow the Holy Spirit to do the surgery needed to restore the soul to a place of health and strength for the journey.

Chapter Four

Follow the Leader

When the Great Shepherd of our souls, with the help of His earthly body, has sufficiently nourished us and brought us through a healing process to restore our souls, He informs us that He has some very special adventures prepared for us. He will take us on a journey where we will see and do new things that we have never seen and done before. We are to travel light as He will provide for us as we go. There will be places of danger and attacks from the enemy, but He assures us that He has everything under control.

It was the ministry of the evangelist that informed us that we could be saved from the mouth of the wolves, and introduced us to our Shepherd. Then the pastors and teachers nourished us with the Word and the Spirit and healed us of our festering wounds. But we move now into the ministry of the prophets and apostles, who impart to us a sense of destiny and Kingdom adventure that takes us to the next spiritual level.

None of us were designed just to stay close to the green pastures and quiet waters. Neither were we designed to take up residence in the "Soul Restoring Care Center." We were designed for adventure, war and conquest. It is the ministry of the prophet and apostle to motivate us to want it. Of course, it will be our Heavenly Shepherd who guides us all the way to our final destiny, but He uses all the ministries that He has given the church to help us get to where we need to go.

Our Heavenly Shepherd exposes us to the radical spiritual activists who insist that God has a plan and destiny for our lives. They speak of gifts and talents and weapons of war that God has given us. They tell us that our weapons are mighty and will pull down strongholds of the enemy.

They also tell us that we will need to die to our personal ambitions, plans and comforts. They will pull out the security blanket from our hands and push us to the edge of the cliff and tell us to trust the Lord. They inform us that the only way to walk into this awesome destiny is to die well and stay close to the Shepherd who will always be there for us.

As we begin this journey into paths of righteousness, we are sure we can do this with no problem. We are in love with the Shepherd. He has done so much for us. He has healed us and forgiven us and given us a love for others. As long as He is there we will be fine.

Soon we find ourselves in new adventures that are pretty exciting. But very quickly we discover that we messed up an assignment. Others on the journey point the finger at us and proclaim our guilt. We want to react and defend ourselves. They don't understand. It's not fair! It wasn't really our fault. Then the Shepherd looks at us with those eyes of His. Those eyes! What can we say when we look into those eyes? "I'm sorry, Jesus. I was wrong. Please forgive me!" He forgives; we apologize to the others, and go on.

Day after day we journey. Some days we do pretty good. Other days we feel like such failures. What's wrong with this picture? Why is there still so much flesh? Why do we have to be corrected so often?

It's called "Discipleship." We are called to walk in paths of righteousness. This is not something we learn in school and get our diploma or degree just by passing a written test. We have to take the "road test." And every little infraction is noticed and dealt with.

One aspect of the "road test" is becoming part of a ministry team. It may be a worship team or a teaching ministry team. It may be a traveling ministry team, but for some reason we get put on a team with the wrong people. Somehow, whoever put this team together didn't notice the problems these people on my team have. They can get very irritating.

Some team members love to talk. Don't they know that people don't really care that much about who said what to whom and how this one reacted to that one? And why do they think that everyone else wants to listen to them while they monopolize the conversation?

Other team members have some really nasty habits, like clicking their pen incessantly. Some have lousy hygiene and you can smell them coming. Some of them have problems with anger and others are so sensitive, you always have to watch what you say for fear they will take offense.

You know, walking the Christian walk wouldn't be nearly so

bad if you didn't have to do it with other Christians. I love Jesus, but I sure have problems with some of my siblings.

Sounds like family, doesn't it? But Jesus is leading us in paths of righteousness, which also means justice. He is teaching us His own standards of justice. That is: You don't get what you deserve and that's such a good thing. You get what He paid for—forgiveness. But He wants us to learn to forgive like He does. He wants us to see justice and righteousness like He does. It's all about mercy, love and forgiveness. He gave it to us and now He is teaching us to give it to others.

Oh yes, He knows it hurts. But He is making us into mighty warriors. He is maturing us in His "Boot Camp" and preparing us for the front lines. It takes a lot of love flowing through our lives to combat the hate arrayed against us coming from people whom Jesus died for. It takes His discipline, empowered by love, to squelch our own natural impulses to return evil for evil. But love is a power like no other and He is teaching us to love like He does.

Focusing on our Leader

The wonderful thing about the journey on paths of righteousness is that our Leader is walking with us and if we focus on Him, we can always know what He wants us to do, because He has walked the pathway before us. Even as Jesus said that He only did what He had seen the Father do, we can do what we have seen Jesus do if we keep our eyes on Him and not on our circumstances.

This will become extremely important as we move into the part of the journey where we walk through the dark valleys of life. We can't walk it by looking at our friends and trying to imitate them. We can only walk it by looking to Him. He is the example and the only One Who has done it right. But He is with us. We can look to Him, the Author and the Finisher of our faith. But more of that later...

Chapter Five

Maturing Our Motives

FOR HIS NAME'S SAKE

We came to Jesus because we realized we needed a Shepherd. Our first experiences with Him involved His giving us security (I shall not want), providing nurture, rest and refreshing (green pastures and still waters), and healing our wounds (restoring our souls). But when we look at the next level, which we just covered in Chapter Four, we discover that we are walking in paths of righteousness, not for our own sakes, but for His name's sake.

This is a very significant shift in motivation, which deserves a closer look. We come to the Shepherd because of our own need or for our own sake. Everything up to this point has been for us. But following Him in paths of righteousness is all about Him and His Kingdom.

The Gospels are full of Jesus' comments on discipleship. And most of His comments had to do with forsaking everything to follow Him. We are told to forsake family, home and resources. We are told to take up our own crosses to follow Him. He informs us that whoever wants to save or hold on to his own life will lose it, but whoever lets go and gives it all up for Him will surely end up keeping it forever.

Just about everyone we know about, who has made an impact for God, has had to give up something very important and special to him or her. These saints have been through pain and suffering and great personal loss, but they have continued to follow and trust Jesus to work things out for His own glory. The power and anointing has come in response to their willingness to die to their own comfort and personal advantage. They have discovered God's principles of fruitfulness. Unless a grain of wheat falls into the ground and dies, it abides alone, but if it dies it brings forth much fruit. (John 12:24)

Discipleship has incredible rewards. When I was a young preacher, I used to preach hard on discipleship as something we needed to be willing to do as good soldiers of Jesus. I read the words of Jesus and knew that He was asking us to lay down our lives for Him. I was determined that I would do so and get as many others to follow me as possible. What I was really missing is what was obvious to the people Jesus was talking to. I never really thought about the benefits. I just thought about the obligation or responsibility as Christians to lay it all down for Jesus.

People would give almost anything to become the disciple of a Mozart or Michelangelo or Shakespeare. Why? Obviously, because they would be associated with that name and would be known as the disciple of Mozart, etc. People would know that they had been taught and mentored by the famous leader, and it would open many doors to fame and wealth for them.

Becoming the disciple of Jesus was a great honor and privilege for the twelve that He chose. So many more individuals would have desired their position, but only twelve were counted worthy of that honor. Later that honor manifested when the members of the Sanhedrin were amazed at their boldness, knowing they were not educated men, but they noted that "They had been with Jesus" (Acts 4:13). Being His disciples meant that they had learned from Him and had become like Him in so many ways.

At the same time, they were doing the same things that Jesus had done before He ascended to Heaven. The sick were healed, the dead were raised, the demonized were delivered and thousands were converted. Having learned to forsake all and follow Christ had paid off in huge dividends as they led the early Acts church in a powerful season of revival. Not only did they see the powerful miracles and the conversion of multitudes, but huge amounts of finances were laid at their feet and entrusted to them to distribute as they saw fit.

The same principle still holds true in our time. If we forsake all to follow Him for His name's sake, we will find that He will reward us with so much more than we could ever give up for Him. But we cannot put the cart before the horse. We cannot seek the rewards and forget about the cross. We must seek Him and His righteousness, for His name's sake, and then without any selfish effort on our part, all kinds of blessings will be added to us.

It's all about motivation. The heart that pleases Jesus is the heart that says, "I love You because you first loved me." We respond to His agape love with His agape love. We have no other source for love. It doesn't come of our own creation. We can only give Him back what He has given us. And He is asking for all of it. He wants all of our affection and love. Even our love for our family — our spouse and our children — should be given to Him although it is channeled to Him through them and to them through Him. He even asks us to love our enemies with this agape love. When we love them, we are loving Him. When we love the least of His brethren, we are loving Him. Ultimately, all our love must go back to its source – the heart of the Father.

Our normal motivation in life for everything we do, including building relationships, is the hope of getting something back for ourselves. But discipleship teaches us that we can do it all for Him. It's like a soldier who is trained not to look out for his own safety, but the safety of the country he is fighting for. He gives up his own freedom when he joins the military, in order to secure the freedom of His nation. So we, when we enlist in God's army and become His disciple, also surrender our own freedom to secure the freedom of many souls, bringing them into the Kingdom of Heaven.

But of course, maturing our motives may not happen instantly when we sign up for the journey. Much more likely, it will happen through a process of discovery. That is, we discover the impurities in our motives. We do so many things that are good, but we so often have mixed motives. Yes, we want to help the poor, but we also want to get a little credit from others for our "unselfish" actions.

We will serve in the choir and give up some of our free time to practice, but we hope that the choir director will notice how well we sing and maybe give us a solo part. We will give our tithes and a little extra, but maybe that will give us a little influence with the leaders when there is a decision to make. We will show hospitality and have people over for a meal, but we really hope they think we are an excellent host or hostess and will compliment us on the meal and the entertainment we provided.

The Shepherd does not want to overwhelm us by showing us all of our flesh at one time, so He gently points out these impurities one at a time as they manifest on the journey. A lot of these revelations will come through the relationships He blesses us with.

Marriage is, of course, His favorite tool to teach us how impure our motives really are. First He lets us choose the person that we think would be the most wonderful in all the world to live with. Then He allows us to make solemn vows in front of all our family and friends who are asked to be witnesses to these vows. Of course the vows we make seem fine and acceptable the day we make them, but what happens after the vows have been made is hard to figure out.

For most people, including Christians, the person we married turns out to be somewhat different than the person we thought we were marrying. It seems that someone substituted Leah for Rachel and we got someone we hadn't planned on marrying. But that's okay. If we learn to love her (or him) and work on it for seven years, maybe she will turn into the Rachel that we thought we were marrying in the first place.

At any rate, God can so wonderfully use our spouse to reveal our own motives that if we pay attention and listen to each other, we won't really need a lot of other sources to reveal our impurities. Spouses have such a natural way of doing it. But rejoice that God has provided this opportunity to learn to die within the four walls of our homes, so He doesn't have to embarrass us in front of the world. Of course, that's another option if we don't allow Him to use those closer to home.

Remember the goal is to become like Jesus. The Christian's life is designed to help us die to flesh so we can live in the Spirit. We want His power, authority and fruitfulness. It won't come without getting pruned. "Agree with your adversary quickly", could easily be applied in many marriage relationships. It's good advice if we want to save a lot of pain in the discipleship process—following Jesus in paths of righteousness.

Chapter Six

Valleys and Shadows

When Life Gets Scary

The "Yea" in "Yea, though I walk" is not a cheer. It doesn't mean we have looked forward to this and finally it's happening. But the "yea" does mean "YES." It is a very positive response to something very negative. It is like saying, "I am fully committed to what I am about to say."

David went through many valleys. He knew what he was talking about. He had spent a lot of time running from Saul through hills and valleys and in caves. His valleys were places where he was exposed to the enemies. They were the places you had to go through to get to where you wanted to go.

The word "valley" in Psalm 23 could be translated "gorge," or "valley with steep mountains on either side." These mountains would be covered with vegetation and inhabited by wild animals, who were observing everything that passed through the valley. You didn't want to spend too much time in the valley, but sometimes you had no choice but to walk through it.

The point that we have usually missed in looking at this Psalm is that, if it represents our spiritual journey, we are in the valleys, not by some accident, or because our enemy brought us there; we are in the valley because we are following our Shepherd, who is leading us in paths of righteousness. Yes, I am saying that it is our own Shepherd who has chosen the path and if we are following Him as His sheep, He will lead us through some of these valleys.

Notice how the phrases follow one another in the psalm. "He leads me in paths of righteousness for His name's sake. Yea, though I walk through the valley of the shadow of death." He, our loving Shepherd, leads us in paths of righteousness and even when those paths of righteousness lead us through the valley of the shadow of death, we will fear no evil.

These valleys are called the "Shadow of Death" for a reason. Where there is a shadow, there is something close by that has made the shadow. But where there is a shadow, there also has to be a light shining. Those are two very important truths to remember.

The enemy of our souls, and of the Kingdom of Heaven, will always try to cast a shadow on our path. He will not be far off from us. And when we are in the valley, a low place in our lives, he will be lurking around, looking for an opportunity to devour us completely.

Our enemy is the personification of death. His shadows speak of death and destruction. It can be a very scary experience if we focus on the shadows. We can totally lose sight of the fact that our Shepherd is still with us. We can easily forget the fact that the shadow is made because there is still a light shining for us that has not gone out.

Your valley may be different than mine. Sometimes my valley will have to do with finances. From the looks of things, I'm going to die financially and be consumed by debt or loss. But that's just the shadow. A shadow can't harm you, and there has to be a light for there to be a shadow.

Sometimes the valley may be sickness in the family. Cancer can be a scary shadow. When I was about forty-three years old, we discovered I had colon cancer. But it was only a shadow of death. There was a simple operation and because of God's power and the wisdom He had given to us earlier about nutrition, there were no complications and no spreading of cancer into the rest of my body, and no treatments necessary. Now many years later, there has been no reoccurrence and I am still alive and doing as much harm to the enemy as possible. That cancer was only a shadow, not death itself.

For some the shadow may be the tragic death or some other disaster of others we are close to. Death came close to us, but we are still alive. We need to see the light which is still shining and learn what our Teacher has for us, as His disciples, to learn from it all.

But another meaning of the "Shadow of Death" is the "dying" that occurs to the flesh in this valley. It's when things get really scary that we have the most intimate heart-to-heart talks with Jesus. It's when we are at the end of our rope that we make our most solemn vows and promise Him that we will die to our personal desires and ambitions, if He will only have mercy on us and deliver us and answer our prayers.

And dying to the flesh is really just like the shadow. It seems real, but it isn't. In other words, it may seem like He is asking you to give up so much that you will just die without it. But when you have actually done it and surrendered your treasure to Him, you realize it wasn't that hard. You didn't really die. It was just like a shadow that wasn't truly real. Instead, you find yourself enjoying what you would never have experienced if you had hung on to what He asked you to give up.

It would have been easy to say that we couldn't afford to go to Mozambique, where Rolland and Heidi Baker were having revival, when we had so many bills to pay and no guaranteed income while we were gone. It would cost thousands of dollars and meant we would not be doing meetings and receiving offerings to pay the bills. Many things could go wrong (and some did), and we could have come home to a financial disaster.

But if we had given in to fear, we would not have had the incredible experiences that radically blessed us in the presence of Jesus there in Pemba and surrounding villages. I've never, in the comfort and security of the western world, had five or six young men run up to us and ask to become Christians, while we walked through their village. I've never seen several deaf people healed in one night along with a blind person or two in the west. I've never seen crowds of over one thousand people, where over half of them responded to the gospel invitation, in all our days of ministering in the western world.

We could have played it safe and filled our schedule with safer meetings and totally missed the opportunities of a lifetime. If we had feared the shadows, we would have missed the light of the glory of God which was shining so brightly over there. I may also have missed a significant revelation that came to me early one morning in Pemba. When I later released that revelation to our mailing list, it produced an amazing and immediate response, almost all of it being very positive.

Other opportunities we would have missed included speaking to both the group of mission students from around the world and also to the precious native pastors who were there for training to lead churches in their villages. We were also given the opportunity to give personal ministry to almost every staff member at the Pemba Center.

We would have also missed the growth of wonderful relationships with very special people, including some of our own team members we didn't previously know. We were also blessed with opportunities to strengthen our relationship with Rolland and Heidi Baker, as well as many other precious staff members and students of their Holy Given School of Missions.

I can't put a price on what we experienced, nor can the others who served with us. Heart attitudes, western mindsets and practical priorities were radically changed and we see life through different lenses now. But we truly walked through the valley of shadows, with missing luggage, stolen items, sickness, Muslim crowds that could have gotten hostile, and the potential for stress between team members. The shadows were there, but we pressed on into the wonderful light of God's presence and power.

In the next chapter, we will learn the secret of successfully walking through the Valley of the Shadow of Death.

Chapter Seven

No Fear Here

For You Are With Me

We have now come to the heart of Psalm 23. Everything up to this point was to get us to this point. In this chapter, we learn the whole purpose for our spiritual journey, and we will discover the secret keys to unlock the treasure chest of God's blessings. Let's hear what the Good Shepherd has to say to His precious sheep.

Two Choices in the Valley

When we walk through the Valley of the Shadow of Death, we have two basic choices. One is a good idea, but the other will have disastrous consequences. Let's begin by looking at the latter choice.

1. Run Away From the Valley. When we see that we are walking near the skeletons of those who have been devoured in the valley, and when we can smell the vile odor of death all around us, our first instinct may be to run as fast as we can and climb out of this death-trap. That would be a very bad idea.

As we mentioned earlier, the valley is really a gorge with steep mountain walls. To get out of this valley, we would have to climb these walls where the wild animals may be hiding, just waiting for some foolish sheep to wander far enough away from the shepherd. But many Christians have made that choice, angry that the Shepherd would let them go through such nasty situations. Then they choose to try to get out of the valley by themselves as quickly as they can, and discovered before too long that they had made a tragic decision.

2. Run Towards the Shepherd. What then is the right choice? The verse declares, "I will fear no evil for You are with me." The second choice is to get "with Him." In other words, we need to be as "with Him" as we possibly can. We need to cling tightly to His hand and stay as close as possible to His side.

We can run from Him, or we can run toward Him. We will always do one or the other when we go through these valleys. But what a privilege it is to walk so close to Him that we too fear no evil or harm. The closer we get to Jesus the more we become aware of His power and love. Jesus made it very plain, Himself, in Matthew 11:28-30.

After inviting the weary and heavy-laden to come to Him for rest, He then invited them to take His yoke upon them. Then He said, "And learn of Me, that I am meek and lowly in heart, and you will find rest for your souls."

When Jesus says, "Take My yoke," He is saying, walk right beside me and work with me. We are connected and pulling the same load together. What a privilege to be yoked together with Christ. The journey through the valley is not so bad when we are close enough to be pulling the same load together.

When Jesus said, "And learn of Me," He was saying that when we walk at His side, we will be in very close fellowship and we will learn many things about Him that we have never known before. We will discover that He is not proud or arrogant, even if He is the Son of God. Rather, we will find Him to be humble and gentle and easy to love. In fact, I believe we will find that He is not critical of us, but that He actually likes us.

Yes, I believe Jesus doesn't just love us with His Agape love because He is God and He has to. He actually does LIKE us. We actually delight Him with our unique personality and interesting responses to life. We begin to find out how absolutely amazing He is and we truly fall passionately in love with Him.

So what is this valley and this whole journey all about? We've kept it a secret until now. This journey is all about INTIMACY.

Yes, we have been set up! The Shepherd was there to rescue us from the wolves. He was there to lead us to the greenest grass and the purest water. He spent time restoring our souls until we appreciated Him so much that we decided to become His disciples and follow Him to the ends of the earth to build His Kingdom.

And then He led us into the Valley of the Shadow of Death. He did it on purpose. He allowed the devil to do some nasty things to us. What was that all about? Yes, it was a setup. He isn't satisfied with our loyal and sacrificial service. He desperately wants our passionate love.

And He knows that deep inside of us, that is what we want more than anything in this world. How does He know that? He made us. He created that desire within us and He knows nothing but passionate and intimate love with Him will satisfy us.

And so now as we move through this dark valley, we forget to look around at the stone monuments all around us. We don't notice the shadows or the howls of the nearby wolves. We only notice the love in His eyes for us. We hear the soothing sound of His affectionate voice and we long to be lost forever in His limitless love. We hear the beat of His oversized heart and our heart begins to beat at the very same frequency.

It's no wonder that we fear no evil. How can we fear evil when He is so very close? How can it even enter our minds that we might perish, when His hands are so strong and His arms are wrapped around us? The fact is ... He is with us. He is as close as we want to get to Him. He gives us His undivided attention and listens to our hearts. Then He shares the deep emotions of His own heart and His love for every one of His unique and special sheep.

Before we have gone too far into the valley we are actually becoming thankful for the valley. We realize if we hadn't come into this valley, we would never have felt compelled to run towards Him and cling tightly to Him.

We realize the truth expressed in Psalm 46:1. "The Lord is our refuge and strength, a very present help in time of trouble." The valley is a "time of trouble." But that is when our Shepherd is "very present." It's the time when He is the closest to us, because it's the time when we draw close to Him. Psalm 46 also repeats the theme from Psalm 23: "Therefore we will not fear, even though the earth be removed, and though the mountains be carried into the midst of the sea...." Again, we can't fear when God is a very present help. The key is His presence. He is with us.

Intimacy has become an extremely hot topic in today's church.

People we know have had numerous Heavenly encounters and visitations from angels, etc. They all speak to us about the deep and awesome love in the eyes of Jesus and the powerful emotions of the Father's heart. They all want more and more of God and are like long lost lovers, who can't wait to get reunited in the next encounter.

Even those who have not had the more dramatic encounters are experiencing a new sense of intimacy as they spend more and more time in Houses of Prayer, Healing Rooms and in private "soaking" times. By soaking, I mean just resting in the presence of the Lord with worship music and the Word, listening and absorbing His presence and glory. These times often produce a deep awareness of the love of Jesus for them. Emotional and sometimes physical healings take place and affection for Jesus increases steadily.

Leaders such as Mike Bickle direct the people of God to The Song of Solomon. They boldly proclaim that the Holy Spirit is focusing the church on the "Bridal Paradigm." Young and old have begun to spend hours in International Houses of Prayer, which often run 24/7, employing live worship, with interactive prayer and intercession, and a new team taking the lead every two hours.

"Perfect love casts out fear." John, the Beloved, wrote a lot about love. He, himself, was the most intimate disciple of Jesus. He understood the power of love. After the resurrection, he and the other eleven disciples experienced the forgiveness of Jesus. They had committed high treason and forsaken their Commander in Chief in His time of trial. They should have been punished with death. But Jesus forgave them completely and put His Spirit on them. They returned this forgiveness with love. As Jesus informed us, those who are forgiven much love much. (Luke 7:47)

The consequence of complete or perfect love is a lack of fear. The apostles, including John, found the courage to look death in the eye and not flinch. They knew how close Jesus was to them. He had told them, "I am with you always, even to the end of the age" (Matthew 28:20). They knew the meaning of "with," just like David did when he said, "I will fear no evil for You are with me." How awesome it is that He is "with" me! The more intimate I get with Him, the more I am aware of the "with" factor and the less I will fear, poverty, sickness or rejection of men.

The valley is a breeze when He is "with" us and we are aware of it. The more our spiritual senses are activated to "see" and "hear" Him, the more we will be aware of His presence and the less we will fear.

And as we stated before, this is the heart of the Psalm. He is with us and He loves us and He likes us. We are secure in Him, but much more important than that, we are "in love" with Him. That's what He has been up to. He has been romancing us in an unexpected way. But He knows how it will end up and He knows we will thank Him some day, as long as we don't run away from Him.

This reminds me of the dream which a brother in Illinois shared with me the night before I was to introduce Heidi Baker at our conference in Crystal Lake, Illinois. He saw a child crawling happily and fearlessly right towards a coiled cobra snake. He was feeling very anxious for the child as it got closer and closer to the deadly reptile. The child kept crawling until it was practically on top of the snake. Then he heard a voice saying that if the child didn't try to flee from the snake, the snake couldn't bite it. Then he saw a large hand grab the snake by the neck and pull it away.

The Lord gave me the interpretation the next morning a few hours before I introduced Heidi to the crowd. The child represented Heidi and the ministry team that went to Cabo Delgado, a Muslim province in northern Mozambique. She went to the Valley of the Shadow of Death. But she feared no evil, because she knew Jesus had sent her and was with her. She didn't run and the enemy was not able to bite. She stayed close to Jesus and He began to take out the enemy and give her favor with many political leaders.

Heidi wouldn't run from fear of the enemy. She always ran straight towards Jesus and she had no fear when she looked into His eyes. She has been such an example to us in the west, where safety and security are such major concerns. Iris Ministries has faced much persecution and some violent attacks. Heidi has been shot at several times.

The problem for her enemies is that she has no fear of death. She longs to spend more time with Jesus in His presence forever. His perfect love has cast out the fear in her life. One of their leaders was recently beaten to death. But Iris Ministries refused to file charges, forgiving the youths who attacked him. The one youth who was caught and jailed was visited and led to Jesus. The dead leader was raised from the dead in time for Resurrection Day celebrations, and the Valley of the Shadow of Death became the Valley of Resurrection.

Let's seek for that intimacy that He is seeking for us. Let's understand the secret of the "secret place." Psalm 91 declares that the one who lives in the "secret place" of the Most High will dwell under the protective shadow of the Almighty. Many prophetic leaders in recent days have talked about the "secret place." Conferences have been named after this phrase. We would all like to be covered by the Lord's shadow, rather than the shadow of death, but what does it mean to live in the "secret place"?

I have a very profound definition of the "secret place." It's a lot like the definition of a stronghold. A stronghold is a strong hold. A "secret place" is a secret place, a place which is secret and where secret things are kept. God has secrets which He only shares with those He allows into His "secret place."

I propose that we all have a secret place. It's the place where we keep our secrets. We have secrets that we don't want anyone to know about. Some secrets relate to our shame for things we have done. Others are dreams and visions that people might not understand. So whom do we let into our secret place? It's usually only those whom we totally trust—in other words, our very best friends.

God has a secret place where He keeps His secrets for His true friends. And who are His true friends? Scripture says that if we want friends, we must show ourselves friendly (Proverbs 18:24). Those who accept the friendship of Jesus and trust Him to come into their own secret place will be considered His friend and allowed into His secret place.

Let me surprise you with an interesting fact from Scripture. Many have memorized part of II Chronicles 16:9 which talks about the eyes of the Lord searching for those to whom He can show His power. What He is looking for is the right kind of heart. Some versions say "perfect or complete," some say "loyal" and some have other variations of those meanings.

The Hebrew word *shalem* actually does mean complete, (figuratively or literally), but then Strong's Concordance dictionary says "especially friendly." The word "friendly" is also the meaning of *shalam* the root word of this word *shalem*.

So the correct meaning could actually be "friendly." God is looking for a friendly heart. What would that mean? As we just discussed, we share our secrets with only our best friends. I believe God will share His secrets with those who have a friendly heart— that is those who will open up every part of their heart and life to Him; those who will commit their lives to Him and make covenants with Him like David did with Jonathon.

In other words, God is looking for a heart that longs for intimacy as much as He longs for intimacy. He is looking for a heart just like His. That is the heart that is complete and friendly. His heart is looking for intimacy. He is looking for others who are looking for intimacy as well. Those will be protected under His shadow, and they will be set free from fear.

We won't have to stay too much longer in the Valley of the Shadow of Death. Just one short chapter to go and we will be singing a different song. So let's move on and see what our Bridegroom has for us.

Chapter Eight

Instruments of Comfort

His Rod and His Staff

As we walk with Jesus through the Valley of the Shadow of Death, we learn to trust Him, and we are given opportunities to serve Him as we walk with Him. He allows us to notice the needs of the other sheep and some of those who have never accepted Him as their Shepherd. As long as we stay close to Him, He gives us the freedom and encourages us to take His love to them.

He also allows us to notice and enjoy some of the beauty that we didn't first notice in the valley because of our fear. Soon our senses are being delighted by the beautiful wild flowers and shrubs that grow in the valley. We notice the beautiful birds and listen to their sweet songs. The bubbling brook has a melody of its own that speaks of tranquility and peacefulness.

We know we are still in that valley that we feared so much. We know others have died here and there is still danger, but we do know that our Shepherd is keeping a watchful eye on us. And even though we'd love to just focus on Him as our Lover, He has invited us to help Him bring His love to others besides ourselves. It would seem very selfish to stay with Him and ignore the others that He also loves. So we walk through life with this constant tension between wanting to be only with Him and wanting to please and serve Him by sharing His love with others.

The Shepherd carries a couple of sticks with Him. One is called a rod and the other a staff. Both of these can be walking sticks.

The word "rod" has a variety of meanings. The rod can be used as a weapon, an instrument of punishment or as a walking stick. It has the more negative connotation.

The word "staff" comes from a word meaning support. It is a support as a walking stick, but it can also be a support for a sheep that needs a helping hand.

So how do these Shepherd's sticks provide us with comfort? I'm very glad you asked that question.

As we begin to work and enjoy our freedom that comes when the fear leaves, we sometimes forget to be cautious. We are still in a valley full of danger, even though it is a beautiful place. We can so easily get distracted and begin to wander in search of new delights and adventures. But the Shepherd never takes His eyes off of us. And we want Him to warn us and correct us if we get too far away from Him.

We know that His rod is for our protection. Sometimes we may need a "Direction Correction." That rod can be used as gently or as firmly as needed to help us get back on the right path and going in the right direction. We know He won't hurt us unless we really need it to save us from disaster. It is in effect a very comforting symbol, reminding us that He won't let us wander too far from His presence.

Direction corrections come in many forms. Sometimes it's a hurtful comment from someone. We don't like it, but it makes us think about our priorities, our attitudes and our devotion to Jesus. It makes us cry out to Him and desire His comfort. Other forms of direction correction can be a lack of finances, sickness, accidents, etc. None of them will be more than we can bear and all of them will steer us back to the pathway of blessing and joy.

The other wonderful thing about the rod is that it is a powerful weapon against our enemies, should we find ourselves threatened by them. It was the rod that saved James in the beginning of this adventure. It will be employed on our behalf many times before the journey is over. The enemy will get too close for his own good, and our watchful Shepherd will make him sorry for that indiscretion.

The staff, which is often pictured with a hook on the end, is another instrument of comfort. We know that if we ever get into a difficult situation where we can't get back on our feet, He will be there with His staff to rescue us. It is an instrument of comfort and support.

Many of us have seen the classic painting of a shepherd reaching out with his staff to rescue a sheep, which is stuck in a precipice of some kind. The sheep has no possibility of getting out of its difficult situation without the help of its shepherd. It is a reminder that we also need our Shepherd. We too get into situations from which we could never extricate ourselves. But how often has Jesus, our Shepherd delivered us from the snare or the pit that the enemy has prepared for us? I know that for me it's more than I can count.

I remember not many months ago that I was in a hurry and found out I had gone too far on a particular road. Not seeing any cars coming, I made a U-turn. Half way through the U-turn I saw a car just a few feet away and barreling towards me at high speed. It should have hit me, but somehow it seems like he just passed through the back of our car without touching it. My Shepherd must have stretched out His staff and pulled me out of the way. Of course He often uses angels for that kind of rescue, according to Psalm 91.

It's good to know that the Shepherd is watching over us. He gives us a great journey through the Valley of the Shadow of Death, once we overcome our fear. The fact is most of our Christian journey has been in that valley. We are always close to death. People we love fall prey to cancer, heart disease and fatal accidents. And we have to die to our ridiculous flesh all the time. For some of us it almost becomes our "comfort zone" to be going through crises.

But our Shepherd is "with us" and He always has His instruments of comfort with Him to help us. He gives us songs in the night and light in the darkness. He gives us peace in the midst of war and joy in our pain. We can live in a supernatural realm, because He is a supernatural God.

So we, His people, and the sheep of His pasture, walk on with Him through the Valleys, singing praises to Him and loving Him with a deep and profound love. We find every opportunity to serve Him because we love Him so much and passionately desire to bless Him.

We give Him thanks for everything He does for us, including the occasional direction correction, and we appreciate the vision and hope that He has given us. We know that we have a destiny, because He has been telling us about it.

In our journey, the Shepherd uses many ways to communicate with us. The chief means of communication is the Bible. But

He also chooses to use prophetic people, including "babes" to speak words of wisdom, edification, exhortation and comfort. He speaks through circumstances, angelic beings (sometimes un-awares) and visions and dreams. But He does speak. And we can hear when we listen. We do recognize His voice, because we are after all His sheep (John 10).

And now we move on to another whole phase of the journey. We can call it the "Reward Phase."

Chapter Nine

Unexpected Honor

It's been a long journey through the Valley of the Shadow of Death. It took some time to walk through it. But the important thing is that we do go "through" it. It didn't come to stay; it "came to pass."

This valley can represent our whole walk with Jesus on the earth, followed by our rewards in Heaven, but it can also represent many cycles of valleys followed by times of rewards. We will focus mostly on these recycling events of valleys and rewards. We all know that Jesus has prepared a place for us in Heaven and that the rewards for serving Him will be very much "out of this world." But we also need to be reminded that even here on earth we see the wonderful hand of God moving miraculously on our behalf to let us know how much He loves us and to give us a foretaste of our Heavenly reward.

He Prepares a Table

When we begin to emerge from the gorge we have called the Valley of the Shadow of Death, we see a broad plain with wonderful vegetation, well cultivated and full of fruit. There are no more bush-covered hills to hide our enemies, and there is a sense of safety and security. It is no longer a lonely place; it is like coming from the wilderness into civilization. In fact there are multitudes of our family and friends, who have been waiting for us to emerge from the darkened valley.

At this point in the story, let me personalize this part of the passage for you.

Soon your Shepherd leads you to a lovely park area. In the center of this park is a beautiful canopy, under which is a pure white table, covered with an exquisitely decorated cloth. At the table are two gold-covered plush chairs. Jesus asks you to sit in one of the chairs while He goes about bringing the feast to the table. Then you notice that you are wearing a beautiful white robe. It is so intricately designed and embroidered with golden thread that you are amazed by it.

After setting the table perfectly and bringing the delicious food and drink to the table, Jesus sits down with you and blesses the feast. Now other gracious servers in beautiful garments attend your every need, so you and Jesus can focus on fellowship.

Other members of your family and faithful friends are seated at nearby tables, to honor you. They are like wedding guests and you and Jesus are the bride and Groom. Everyone is ready to celebrate, but you have a hard time taking your eyes off of Jesus.

Finally, you begin to notice other people watching this feast from a distance. Among them are some of the people who have been thorns in your flesh along the way. Some have been down-right nasty and some have persecuted you for your faith in God. Others said that you'd never make it on your journey. They had ridiculed you and told you that you'd be back to your old life-style within weeks. Now they are watching as you partake of a scrumptious meal with the King of Kings and Lord of Lords in the center of the park.

Finally Jesus rises and speaks loudly to all. He declares that this is a time to celebrate and honor one who has been a faithful servant, passing through the great and dangerous valley. He tells the whole world that He has come to know you in a very special way and that He and you have become such good friends that He is delighted to honor you on this very important occasion. Then He lifts His wine glass and declares a toast to His faithful bride and friend.

The crowd cheers, claps and whistles. Trumpets sound, sym-bols clash and someone plays an energetic and explosive drum roll. Jesus smiles and looks deeply into your eyes and communi-cates infinite, powerful love and affection. The tears begin to roll down your cheeks.

You don't really understand it. All you did was follow your Shepherd and cling to Him for protection. You allowed Him to correct you, but you knew that was just His love for you. You had obeyed His voice, but that was in your best interest, as well. So now, for reasons you don't begin to understand, He has actually prepared this amazing banquet, and you are His honored and special guest.

But it is true. Jesus allows us to go through the valleys, but He will always prepare a reward for our faithfulness and love. Not that His love is not reward enough, but He always has to go way beyond the call of duty. He will always out-love us, out-give us and out-serve us. He is the King, but He has chosen to be our Servant as well.

My wife, Brenda, worked on a surgical team in our small town, where we were pastoring a church and Christian school which we had pioneered. The hospital staff had the normal pecking order, typical of most institutions. Brenda had taken a course as a surgical tech while I finished seminary, and although she had always dreamed of being an R.N., she was just happy to be working in a hospital and enjoyed surgery very much.

Various doctors and nurses came and went in that hospital, but everyone knew the pecking order. The best surgeons were at the top, general practitioners were way up there as well, registered nurses were next to them, and then all the LPNs, technicians, etc., were servants to them. Of course, after that came the other services, such as laundry and janitorial services, which were at the bottom of the heap. Basically, it had to do with the amount of knowledge, education and income that each person had.

There were many times that Brenda would find herself in situations where those over her would pull rank and actually take advantage of her, or put blame on her that she didn't deserve. Of course, if a surgeon said it was her fault, then it was her fault. You didn't argue with a surgeon. That would be like a Catholic person accusing the Pope to his face.

In such situations, Brenda always had to talk to the Lord and get her encouragement from Him, because often those over her would only care about their own reputation and income. But God had put her in a position of learning to love those who took advantage of her and doing her best to serve them even when things weren't fair. Techs and other lower folk on the totem pole seldom got complimented. They just did what they were told to do and tried to keep their superiors from finding something to criticize.

But one day one of the surgeons was attempting to get certified to do a type of surgery for which he was not previously certified. This involved performing several surgeries under the watchful eye of two visiting surgeons, who had the task of certifying surgeons in the state of Washington. This particular surgeon, who wanted the certification, often used foul language and could be quite rude and hurtful, but he was a surgeon and no one would call him on it.

The day came for his big test, and Brenda was a bit nervous, because she would be closely watched as well, even though she was not applying for any certification. The surgical team did three back-to-back surgeries that day. When they all finally took off their masks one of the professors turned to Brenda and said to them all, "This lady is one of the best surgical techs we have ever observed. She does an outstanding job."

Brenda was a bit overwhelmed. This was not what she was used to. But in front of all her critics and supervisors, Jesus had spread a table for her. Jesus had announced to all those in the room that she was His beloved, and that He was well-pleased with her.

As a team, we have experienced the "table of honor" on numerous occasions, especially right after going through a valley. Financial valleys are common to traveling ministries, who depend on the favor of God and man for their income. But we have seen God honor us for trusting Him by sudden surprises from Heaven, using other precious saints to bless us with delightful gifts.

Jesus delights in honoring every child of His that shows love and faithfulness towards Him. Sometimes we have done so little for Him that it is hard to understand, but He reminds us that He is not grading our activities; He is looking deep into our hearts to see how much desire and love for Him is there that He can reward. He is an awesome Shepherd; He is an awesome God.

Chapter 10

A New Anointing

After enjoying being the guest of honor at the banquet table, Jesus takes you to a place in a beautiful garden under a majestic, towering tree with huge branches. Under the shade of this tree He takes a large flask of oil.

You kneel at His feet and weep softly in gratefulness for His kindness to you. You understand the oil. This is anointing oil. It is what you have earnestly desired. You have wanted more power to serve Him. You have wanted more power to bless people in need. He is about to pour this oil out on your head, and all you can do is weep.

Then with head bowed, you feel the warm oil begin to touch your head. Little by little it begins to flow down onto the beautiful garment He has given you, although it leaves no stain at all. You stay on your knees for some time, while He speaks softly to you. He declares that He is anointing you to preach the good news, to set captives free and to bring healing and hope to a hurting people.

You finally rise to your feet and are very much aware that you are carrying a brand new anointing. Although other things may look and feel the same, there is something different in the way you interpret what your senses are telling you. There is a new faith that within you lies a power that can change your world and the worlds of many other people. You hold things inside like Mary after the angel spoke to her and you ponder them in your heart.

Soon you find yourself encountering someone with a real and troubling need. Within you there arises a surge of anger at the enemy for hurting someone that God created to bless. Spiritual discernment has increased and you can see what the enemy has done and the stronghold that he has built. As faith rises in your spirit, you tear down the stronghold, rebuke the afflicting spirit and bring freedom and blessing to one troubled soul. Jesus whispers to you, "I created you for this and much, much more."

Brenda has always been an encourager. Even as a child, she would befriend the least accepted girls in school. They may have been mentally slow or physically handicapped, but Brenda made them her friends. She just felt compassion and was always wanted to make them feel better.

When we began our ministry, she didn't know much about co-pastoring a church, but she did know how to make people feel loved and important. She always attracted some of the most spiritually needy people, who had been rejected by others, but she did her best to help them become victorious in their life with many encouraging and loving words.

In addition to encouraging adults, Brenda has always had a strong love for children. And as many pastor's wives have discovered, not many people feel "called" to the nursery or children's ministries. So you know where she spent a lot of her time in those almost thirty years of pastoral ministry. In addition to nursery, Sunday School and Children's Church, she also served as girls club leader and phonetics teacher in our Christian school.

Wherever Brenda served, whether children or adults, she tried to make everyone feel loved and special. It was not something she had to work at too much, but she always found something nice to say or a surprise gift to give. Everyone wanted to be her special friend and she made each of them feel so loved and accepted that they felt like they were her very best friend. Of course, there were some who put unreasonable and unhealthy expectations on her. There were those who abused her generosity in various ways. And, of course, there were those who attacked her when they discovered that she was a human being with weaknesses of her own. Personal attacks really hurt her deeply, as she always wanted to make things better for others, and couldn't understand how others could attack with such anger and vindictiveness.

But Brenda would still do her best to help people feel better and she would encourage others with compliments. She kept serving the kids and the young women who had more problems than any soap opera character that ever existed. She had emotional trauma and insecurities of her own from some past experiences, but she never stopped trying to help others find joy and fulfillment in life.

Brenda has spent a lot of time in the Valley of the Shadow of Death. Some of the time she has been dying to her desires and comforts and to her flesh. But a lot of the time she has been helping others walk through their valleys. Often Jesus asks His children who have already been through that valley to be His visible representative and make Him real to the person going through the valley. My wife knows how to weep with those who weep as well as rejoice with those who rejoice.

After almost thirty years of pastoral ministry, we moved into a transition time of life, being about fifty years old. We spent some time in another ministry absorbing the training in the prophetic realm that was being taught and exampled. We didn't know where God was leading us next, but something unusual began to manifest.

I had always considered myself more of a prophet than my wife, since I had been raised in it and felt called to speak for the Lord in one way or another, and since my wife really didn't ever prophesy. But other prophets began to prophesy to her that she was going to explode into the prophetic.

During some of the training sessions, she was invited to come to the front and pick out people to prophesy to them. Everyone was amazed as the prophetic anointing fell on her with power. After seeing a few examples, one of the leaders invited us to serve at a pastor's retreat in Canada with them. I shared a teaching on unity and Brenda was turned loose for a few minutes to prophesy.

Again she exploded with prophetic words over several people, one of whom was a pastor's wife who would shortly lose her son to a Columbine-style shooting in Tabor, Alberta. God turned that tragedy to great good and the word that Brenda gave her of working with many youth turned out to be very true. The pastor and his wife both were on national television sharing their testimony. After that, they had an incredible open door to many young people, as well as desperate parents.

As they say, "The rest is history." As we began to travel, Brenda would prophesy to person after person with an unusual, strong and accurate prophetic anointing. I often point out to people that she was so faithful to encourage people before she had a prophetic anointing, that God gave her the supernatural gift so she could edify, exhort and comfort with more power and efficiency. She had been faithful to encourage with a heart of love and compassion and God took her to the next level and poured the anointing oil all over her.

Brenda had spent much time in the valleys, but her day came for the release of the anointing that was part of the "reward package." As of today she has probably prophesied to over thirty thousand people since those first days of prophetic training and ministry. No one goes faithfully through the valleys, clinging to Jesus and getting to know Him, without ending up with a greater and stronger anointing to serve Him.

As I said above, I had always thought that I was the prophet in the family. It had been spoken over me that I would prophesy, and I had felt that strong anointing at times. But prophecy had never been my strongest gift. Instead, I became Brenda's helper in this ministry, which was a reversal of our previous thirty years of ministry. She had been my helper as we had served the Lord in four different churches. She had never felt very secure in the ministry, not having the background that I had in Scripture and the church.

But today, God has increased the anointing on both of us. We know a little more about where we fit and what our giftings are. We don't compete with each other, we complete each other. We both know how much better off we are together than apart. Where I am weak, she is strong and where she is weak, I am strong. It's the same anointing oil, but it empowers different gifts in our lives.

We have both been through the valleys with Jesus. We have stumbled and strayed at times, but we have always responded to His direction corrections, and we have humbled ourselves and asked for His mercy and grace to go on. We have apologized many times to many people, including our children. We have responded to the altar calls of many revivalists and evangelists, asking God for more of His power and anointing.

In response, God has visited us and we have experienced some wonderful special times in His presence. Some visitations have brought physical healing. Others have brought awesome revelations, and others have brought strong encouragement and vision for our destiny.

The wonderful thing about the anointing oil, once it has been poured out on us, is that it will never run out as long as we keep pouring it into others. It's only when we stop pouring into others that we start to feel dry and empty. But when we begin to serve others with that wonderful anointing, we feel ourselves filling up again.

God so enjoys giving us the rewards for faithfulness in the valley. So far we have looked at the table of honor which He spreads for us, and the anointing oil which He pours out on us. It's time to move on to the next item on His reward list.

Chapter Eleven

Incredible Prosperity

MY CUP RUNS OVER

You have been the guest of honor at Jesus' banquet. You've been anointed for a ministry of power. But today, Jesus wants to affirm His love for you in another way. He has walked with you through the valley and become your dear Friend. He knows that at this point you are ready and able to receive the blessings you previously desired, but weren't ready to handle. Now, like Solomon, your heart desires just to be able to serve Him, love Him and bring joy to His heart. You are not asking for many great things for yourself. Rather, your desires are all for Him.

But Jesus bids you follow Him again. Now He is leading you to a huge and palatial warehouse. He opens the door and invites you in. The room is instantly lit up by His presence and you gasp in awe and amazement.

Before you on hundreds or thousands of velvet-covered tables are the most beautiful gems and pearls you have ever seen. At the side of the endless room are huge treasure chests full of money from every nation on earth. Huge piles of gold bars are stacked beside the money chests. Nothing on earth can even begin to compare.

Jesus gives you a very large basket covered on the outside with beautiful living flowers. He whispers to you, "Let's see if we can fill this up." Then He leads you to table after table and picks out the very items that catch your attention as soon as you see the table. He reaches into the money chests and picks up bundles of bills of great value from several different countries, and you know that you will be going to those places with His anointing before too long.

Then He picks up several gold bars and comments, "You can use these anywhere." You smile in agreement, still in total awe and almost unable to speak.

Suddenly it occurs to you that all these gemstones and gold bars should weight a ton in your basket. But the basket still feels as light as it did empty. Jesus knows your thoughts and jokes, "Didn't I tell you that My burden is light?"

You laugh out loud and suddenly your emotions are released. Tears of joy come flooding out of your awestruck eyes, momentarily blinding you, and you break out into uncontrollable sobbing. Your sense of unworthiness is overwhelming you, and you feel the arms of Jesus surrounding you with His love.

His soothing voice penetrates your innermost being. "I know you don't feel worthy, precious child, but I have found you faithful and true. Your heart of love for me makes me want to bless you. I delight in giving you more than you think you deserve."

His embrace and loving words bring great comfort and then He instructs you to look at your basket. It is truly full and overflowing with the most beautiful of treasures and wealth. You understand what He said, but still you don't comprehend the vastness of His love, power and resources.

He leads you back out of the treasure house and speaks to you again. "I have blessed you with this overflowing basket for two reasons. First of all, I delight in you and want to show you the greatness of my love. But secondly, I have much for you to do in my name and I want you to have all the resources you need. I don't want you holding back in serving me because of fear of lack. You won't always see this basket in the places I send you, but know that it is always available for you when you really need the resources."

"Some of the jewels you will give as gifts to show others my love. You will never run out. Give them freely as I direct you. You will use the money I give you to build my Kingdom in many nations. Listen for my still small voice. Sometimes the amounts I instruct you to give will seem impossible, but just remember what you have seen today. I will never exhaust My treasure house by giving to you and others like you."

You nod in agreement. You will never ever forget the scene inside that incredible place. It will be indelibly etched into your mind forever. You are more than ready to begin the journey of ministry, wherever He calls you. There is a huge, enormous, gigantic "YES" in your spirit.

When David said, "My cup runs over," he was referring to blessings of all kinds. The cup often referred to destiny and either blessing or pain. Some had to drink a cup of suffering and shame, while others like Nehemiah drank wine from the king's own cup. We may taste from the cup of pain in the valley, but the reward will always be an overflowing cup of blessing when we graduate from each valley experience.

Not too long ago, while still living and traveling full time in a motor home, we were given prophetic words that said we would have a brand new motor home. One person had actually seen the inscription, "Diesel Pusher" on it. He claimed he had never heard of a diesel pusher, but we already knew that's what we needed to go over the mountains of western North America.

We had also been given words like, "Where's all this money coming from?" In addition, I had seen a quick vision of myself sitting on the floor (representing my past poverty), and there was a pile of gold nuggets in front of me. Suddenly, a stream came out of the pile of gold and began to completely cover me in gold. I liked what I saw, but didn't know the meaning of it.

Before long, through a series of circumstances, large amounts of money began coming in to our bank account from a dear friend who had lost his wife a month or two before. He had begun to close her bank accounts and sent us a portion of each account. When he was done, we found we had just enough money in our account to close the deal on the brand new diesel pusher we had made a deposit on by faith.

Then this gentleman invited us to his house and began to give us some of the jewelry that his wife had accumulated in her jewelry business. It was all real gems and real gold. Brenda was given a lot of rings and chains, etc. that she was given to bless others with, especially pastors' wives. We saw a lot of tears of joy as the Holy Spirit instructed Brenda to give certain rings to certain women. For many of them it was their birthstone or it had some other special significance to them.

Then our friend pulled out a few men's items. He gave me a couple of gold rings with diamonds and a watch. It looked like just a nice watch, but when I read the label it read, "Rolex." It was made with eighteen carat gold. I had never worn any jewelry but a simple plain wedding band and cheap Wal-Mart watches. Suddenly, it was like I was covered in gold.

We could truly say, "Our cup is full and running over!" The motor home was awesome. We got the previous year's model, so it was reduced substantially in price, but had all the features we really wanted for our family of four with two growing teenage boys. Soon it was filled with guitars, keyboards and skateboards, etc. We could only stand back in awe at the goodness and lovingkindness of our Savior and Lord.

Shortly after the purchase of the diesel pusher motor home, we were feeling that the time had come for us also to have a house for our family. We didn't know it, but God was beginning to speak to our single daughter, Andrea, about coming home and spending time with us after five years in Dallas, Texas, which included three years at Christ For the Nations College and some mission adventures in Eastern Europe.

This time we had no cash in the bank for a down payment, so it didn't make any sense to look for a house, but we did anyway. The first day we found there were programs to buy without a down payment and the second day we found the house. We got much more than we dreamed of in a house. It was brand new and had a lot of space, with a bedroom for each of the kids, including Andrea, who came home right when the house became available.

Once again, we saw how God could fill our cup to overflowing with His blessings when we were willing to walk through the valley with Him. The valley, especially for Brenda, was going without a house for five years. We had to kill the flesh and draw closer to Jesus to survive. Brenda had really learned to soak and teach others to do the same through this time. It had been a time of developing intimacy with God.

But oh how God showed us His love and rewards even before the valley was over. After we got the house, we still traveled a lot and made use of the motor home, but we always looked forward to coming home. For us, going home was like taking a vacation is for others. We didn't want to get away, we wanted to come home. But wherever we were, we knew God had honored us, anointed us and filled our cup to overflowing.

And He wants to do the same for you!

Are you ready for the next reward?

Chapter Twelve

Blessed Assurance

SURELY GOODNESS AND MERCY, TRUE ETERNAL SECURITY

This wonderful psalm finishes with a wonderful verse of blessed assurance. What a joy it is to know that our Shepherd loves us so much that He has commanded goodness and mercy to pursue us all the days of our life.

Our youth group (I was a member of one of those not too many decades ago) used to sing the popular chorus, "Surely goodness and mercy shall follow me all the days, all the days of my life," etc. But we (the guys) changed the words a bit and sang "Shirley, Audrey and Laurel shall follow me." Obviously, those were three of the cutest gals in the youth group.

But what God is really saying in this passage is that the journey of discipleship that He leads us on is the way that brings what every human soul is looking for. Everyone wants to have the security of knowing what his or her future is and knowing it with certainty.

When we have been through the valleys with our Shepherd, and when we have walked with Him in close and intimate fellowship, something has taken place in our inner man. We no longer have those nagging doubts that say, "What if I haven't been good enough?" or "What if I mess up in the future?" or "What if I just think I believe?" or "what if I didn't really forgive everyone?" And the list goes on.

But because He has fed us His word and filled us with His Holy Spirit, because he has restored our soul and then taken us triumphantly through the valley, because we learned how much He loves us and likes us, and because He has honored us, anointed us, and profoundly blessed us, all those "what ifs" have been silenced forever. His love has surrounded our entire being, our mind, will and emotions, and our body, soul and spirit. Our heart is totally at peace and rest and we can truly say, "Surely." That means that there is absolutely no doubt about it.

It would help us to visualize Goodness and Mercy as the names of two angels who are assigned to follow us everywhere we go. When we get up in the morning, Goodness and Mercy stretch their wings and get ready to follow us through the day. When we leave the house they join us on our journey influencing people and situations around us to bring goodness and mercy into our lives.

When trials and tests come our way, Goodness counteracts with extra blessings. When we mess up and feel guilty and ashamed for our actions, Mercy intervenes and reminds us of God's love and forgiveness. Whenever we have a need or mess things up, Goodness and Mercy are there to bless and restore.

And David didn't just say they might be there, but he said, "Surely" they would be there. When we obey God and stay close to Him through the hard times, and learn about the desire of His heart for intimacy, He puts that deep and blessed assurance into our spirit in such a way that nothing can shake it. It's not about how we interpret the various Scriptures that say we can be saved and lost again or saved and never lost again. It's about the fact that we know the Author personally. He has put His love deep in our hearts and we cannot fear death, because perfect love has cast out fear forever.

I Will Dwell

The first part of the last verse of Psalm 23 tells about our confidence in the goodness and mercy of God. The second part speaks of the confidence we have as to where we will spend the rest of eternity. The word dwell means to make yourself at home, or more literally, it means to sit down. David said that he would dwell in the house of the Lord forever.

When you walk into someone else's house that you don't know very well, you don't just go and make yourself at home until the host or hostess invites you to do so. But when you come to the place you live, your Daddy's house, you don't need to wait for an invitation. You can go to the living room and sit down, rearrange the cushions, and put your feet up on the coffee table if you like. You can go into the kitchen and check out what's in the refrigerator and the cupboards. You can make yourself a snack and you can take a bath or a shower. You don't need permission because that's where you dwell. It is your Daddy's house and that's where you live. His house is your house.

Let's look a little deeper now at the "house of the Lord," the place we will live forever. Not only does it apply to our Heavenly mansions, but it applies to the House that God is building on earth. As we know from Ephesians 2, we are all stones in that house, which is built upon the foundation of the apostles and prophets, Jesus Christ, Himself, being the Chief Cornerstone.

These stones are alive and covered with the glory of God, like the Old Testament stones were covered with gold. When we say we will dwell in the House of the Lord, it means we are to live as part of that house, as well as in it, together with other saints who have been placed in that house.

Now let's connect that truth to the aspect of our feelings of security or "blessed assurance." Everyone wants to feel like they belong. Our intimacy with God has given us the assurance that not only does God love us, but that we belong with His people, His church and His Kingdom.

We are not only accepted by Him, we have a place in His house, a position to fill, and a gift to use for His glory. We are not just children playing around all day, but we are taking our place, being a blessing to others and helping provide a place of safety for those who are young in the Lord and in need of protection.

We are important for two reasons. The first is who we are, because of Who our Father is. The second is our position or responsibility. God loves us because of who we are, but He also honors us for what we do. The last chapter of Revelation tells us that we will be rewarded according to our works, and we were designed to find fulfillment in our work. God in His infinite wisdom allows us to enjoy our work, both in natural endeavors and in spiritual endeavors. And He allows us to find fulfillment in relationships in both the natural and spiritual realms.

The great wise and omnipotent God and Creator of us all, set in motion His magnificent plan for His creation, and we are benefiting from it today and will for all of eternity. From the green pastures and clear waters, He leads us to the place of intimacy and passion for Him. We serve, endure hardships and develop our abilities and gifts to bless His Kingdom.

Then He surprises us with blessings beyond what we could have imagined. Honor, anointing, prosperity and security are lavished on us. We discover the awesome beauty of His Heavenly palace, which becomes our home, and we continue to explore the incredible beauty of His wonderful heart.

AND IT WILL NEVER, NEVER, NEVER, NEVER, NEVER, NEVER EVER END!!!

Bonus Chapter

Especially for Pastors

Whether you have the chief oversight of a church or you have the "Five-Fold" calling to be a shepherd to some precious sheep, this chapter is for you. If that's not your gift or calling or function, you can read on anyway. Just remember that this information is not designed for fuel for criticism of those God has put over His flock.

In the Same Country

As I mentioned in a previous chapter, I recently had an experience where God downloaded fresh revelation, while driving our motor home on a cross-country journey. I was wishing I had read my Bible before starting out at about 4:00 A.M. I often read a few verses before starting my journey, but I had forgotten to do so this time. The boys were still sleeping in the back bedroom (It was already about 7 A.M.), and my wife was already at our destination, as she had flown to Washington state to be with our daughter, Barbie, who had just given birth to her fourth boy.

I was wishing I could just open a Bible and read a few verses, regretting my oversight at 4 A.M. Suddenly, a verse crossed my mind. It was a verse I may never have intentionally memorized, but it was such a popular Christmas verse, that I knew it by heart. It was from Luke 2 and went like this: "And there were in the same country shepherds abiding in the fields, keeping watch over their flocks by night."

I knew the context of this verse from Luke 2. Right before this verse was the story of Mary giving birth to "Baby Jesus," and right after it we read that an angel, followed by a multitude of the Heavenly host, appeared to the shepherds and the glory of God shone upon them and all around them.

As I was wondering why this verse had gone through my mind, God began to speak to me some very important principles that I was soon sharing at conferences where we were speaking to dozens of pastors. It was a very strong and challenging word for us all.

The phrase, "in the same country," means in the same region —not a political entity. It means they were close to where Jesus was being born.

God was doing something so new and special, something that would forever change the course of history. And they were right where they were supposed to be. Notice the following key points:

1. They were very close to what God was doing. They were not in Jerusalem where the religious authorities were. The Pharisees were sure that anything important to their religion would happen in that "holy city." The shepherds couldn't be in Jerusalem. They were busy taking care of their sheep in Bethlehem. They stayed with their wooly friends and watched over them, and they were blessed for their faithfulness by being in the right place at the right time when Jesus was born. The first awesome blessing was that the glory of God fell on them with an angelic visitation.

These Bethlehem shepherds were already in the "same country," representing those who are called to serve and are faithful to their calling, whether it be pastoring, evangelizing, teaching, prophesying or doing the work of an apostle. They did what they knew they should be doing until they heard the word from the angels. At that point they left their sheep, presumably in someone else's care, and went to where Jesus had been born. They were in the same country, but they wanted to be even closer and see Him with their own eyes. The angelic visitation was an incredible experience, but they were not satisfied with that when they heard that they could actually see Jesus, the Messiah, Himself.

It's interesting that these shepherds, whose job it was to take care of sheep and lambs were the first to see the one and only "Lamb of God." This was a tremendous honor for them. The shepherd's blessing for faithfulness was the coming of the glory of God. The blessing for their obedience to the angelic message was seeing Jesus, Himself.

The wise men, who came from the east, were not already in that place, but they had a hunger for more of God and a desire to be in the "same country" where God was doing something special. As a result, they made a great sacrifice to journey to that place to be there to bless the new King. They also came not only to the "same country," but to Jesus, Himself.

An obvious application is that whatever our place in the Kingdom, we should want to be in the "same country" whenever God is doing something new. But our ultimate desire should always be to see Jesus, Himself. We can never be the same once we have seen Jesus.

Today God is birthing new things very quickly and it takes being spiritually alert to keep up and be in the "same country." If we want to be where the glory of God falls, we need to have that strong passion to be there where He is working in order to participate in what He is doing on the earth. God is so into "new things." Many Scriptures repeat this theme. The final one is in Revelation 21, where He says, "Behold, I make all things new."

Many have criticized those who run to wherever a new revival breaks out, saying they should be faithful at home. There may be a delicate balance between faithfulness to commitments and hunger for revival, but we can be much more of a blessing to those at home if we get some fresh manna from time to time and have a hunger for whatever God has for this present generation. Many denominational leaders over the centuries have missed out because the new wave of revival didn't start with them, and they refused to check it out for themselves, lacking a hunger for God and not wanting to change the status quo.

Many Jews, like Saul of Tarsus, who is now known as the Apostle Paul, may have faithfully stayed in the Pharisee's camp, but others made the effort to go and hear Jesus, because there was a hunger in their hearts for something more. So today, shepherds should be looking for fresh pastures for their sheep. And ultimately, we should be more passionate about knowing Jesus intimately than we are about our own ministry or even our sheep. Our desire to see the King and bless His Kingdom should overshadow our other passions.

2. The shepherds were living out in the fields. They made the sheep a priority, knowing that it was their calling. They gave up the comforts of home to stay close to the sheep. They surely smelled like the sheep and would not have been invited into the inner circle of Scribes and Pharisees, but they did what they were called to do and stayed with their sheep. Of course, as we mentioned above, when the glory of God fell and they heard from the angels, they left their sheep long enough to go see Jesus in the inn.

Pastors (shepherds) need to make the sacrifices to be with their sheep. Serving the sheep is a noble ministry in the eyes of God. I believe God does not want us to disassociate with the sheep and associate only with other shepherds. These shepherds lived right with their sheep and that's where the glory fell.

If however, you are the leader of a larger or growing church and you have great vision and a "Kingdom heart," you may be more of an apostle than a pastor. In such a case you should be choosing and appointing those with true shepherd hearts to watch over the sheep. An apostle must still love the sheep, but he must also spend time with his Commander and with other generals in the army of God. He must be busy discerning God's strategy for the battle and the expansion of the Kingdom.

The same holds true for other ministries such as the prophet, the evangelist and teacher. It you are one of these, but you are leading a local church and called the "pastor," you need to make sure you have people with a true pastoral gifting serving the sheep, while you are faithful with your particular calling.

3. They were with the sheep at night. It was during the darkness of night when all the hungry predators came out, looking for fresh mutton for their families. It was the time of greatest danger. They didn't abandon their sheep when things got dangerous. They were there for them, even if it meant having to confront a lion or bear, as David had done, perhaps in the same fields near Bethlehem.

Perilous times may come again to the church in our lifetime. Our sheep will need to know they can trust us to be there to protect them from the wolves, the lions and the bears. If we are faithful to them, they will "know the sound of our voices" and trust in our advice and wisdom. In many ways, we are and have been in a "night" season, even in the western church. Physical persecution is not that common here, but our society has become increasingly dark as far as spiritual life is concerned. Our sheep need us to guide them through these dark times, while we pray and seek the light of revival.

4. They kept their sheep close to the fire. The only way they could protect their sheep at night would be to keep them as close to the fire as possible. Perhaps they had dogs to help them, but the fire would be their only source of light, and warmth during the cold Bethlehem nights.

Today, it is so crucial that shepherds keep their sheep as close to the fire as possible. Fresh fire has been falling on the people of God, but many in traditional churches are carrying on as if nothing has changed and tomorrow will be just like today. We can't afford not to stay close to the fire. For us that means doing many things, in addition to personal Bible study, soaking and worship time. It includes going to as many key prophetic and teaching conferences as possible, reading cutting-edge books, listening to CD's and tapes and watching videos and DVD's of speakers we can grow from.

It also means the joyful sacrifice of going to places like Mozambique and Korea, where God has been pouring out His revival fire in powerful ways. We go and we take as many people with us as we can. Although we don't "pastor" a church, as such, we find that many people want to join us as we pursue the "fresh manna" or "new wine" that God is pouring out.

Wherever God's fire is falling, we want to be close to it. Whatever God is speaking to His body, we want to be listening. He won't always speak to us directly. He doesn't work that way. He expects us to be listening to each other. In Revelation, He said seven times: "He that has an ear to hear, let him hear what the Spirit says to the churches." Notice it is plural "churches", not church. Paul instructed the Colossians to share their letter from him with the Laodiceans and to read his letter to the Laodiceans in the church of Colosse. (Col. 4:16). God wants His church to be His body and we should always be interacting with one another and updating what God has been saying.

The Local Church

Shortly after the "in the same country" revelation, Brenda and I were in Mozambique with a team of about twenty North Americans. Again I had an experience where a statement went through my mind. It was early one morning and I was just partially awake. It was a statement that had never crossed my mind before, nor did it have a place in my theology.

Common sense would dictate that I shouldn't repeat this statement in a book, especially in a chapter for pastors. I have no desire to offend pastors, since a significant part of our ministry and family income flows through pastors who invite us to speak in their churches. I may be somewhat lacking in wisdom or intelligence, but I am sharing this because of a passion to reach the lost throughout the whole world and build the Kingdom of God.

So please understand that having been in pastoral ministry for about thirty years, I am not trying to insult or offend pastors. I must also say that we are seeing a wonderful trend among pastors and churches to correct the problems we will discuss in the following paragraphs. But please read on and see if you can agree with me that God desires to bring some changes in the way we "do" church.

The statement that I heard was this: "The biggest hindrance to the spreading of the gospel is the local church." What a shocker! It didn't make any sense to me either. I know that "local churches" send and support thousands of missionaries and do street evangelism and soup kitchens, etc., etc.

So what was the Holy Spirit saying to me when He said the local church was the biggest hindrance to the spreading of the gospel? I believe God was shocking me and challenging me to analyze the statement until it made some sense.

I had to study the wording and definitions. First the Holy Spirit focused me on the word "local." Then I had to think of the concept of "spreading the gospel." I also realized that the enemy has never been able to stop the spreading of the gospel, even with persecution. But I realized that almost all Christians are at least somewhat submitted to the vision and philosophy of some "local" church.

Thus that local church has significant control of what individual Christians do with their gifts and callings in the Kingdom, as well as their finances. Therefore if the local church does not foster and promote missions and evangelism outside of it's four walls, it can greatly reduce the amount of missions and evangelism that would occur if they did foster and promote those ministries.

The biggest help in understanding the statement came from studying the word "local" itself. When I finally got to a dictionary on the internet, this is what Webster had to say about the word "local." I have highlighted several significant parts of the definition, which I copied directly from Webster's Dictionary on the internet.

Main Entry: ¹lo·cal
Pronunciation: 'lO-k&l
Function: *adjective*
Etymology: Middle English *localle*, from Middle French *local*, from Late Latin *localis*, from Latin *locus* place—more at STALL.

1 : characterized by or relating to **position in space** : having a **definite spatial form** or **location**.

2a: **of, relating to, or characteristic of a particular place** : **not general or widespread** b : **of, relating to, or applicable to part of a whole.**

3a: **primarily serving the needs of a particular limited district** b *of a public conveyance* : making all the stops on a route.

4 : **involving or affecting only a restricted part of the organism** : TOPICAL

5 : of or relating to telephone communication within a specified area.

95

These definitions are quite interesting. Read them carefully, noticing the concept of "not widespread," "limited" and "restricted." I have often found Webster's definitions to be a great source of understanding and inspiration. Daniel Webster was an amazing Christian and his definitions often reflect it. For instance look up the word "glory" for some great insights.

At any rate, I believe that the term "local church" is not the best term, but unfortunately the definitions of the word "local" do describe our western churches to some extent. Keep in mind that I was there in Mozambique with Rolland and Heidi Baker, where we had just been on several outreaches to villages which were totally Muslim. Most of the people received the Lord. Many powerful miracles happened, accompanied by mass conversions. Churches were being planted frequently throughout the region. I was witnessing the biblical standard of "spreading the gospel."

In contrast, in the western church we often primarily serve the needs of *"a particular limited district."* (See definition above.) Our vision that motivates and drives us as pastors is so often the building of "our" church, not the universal body of Christ or His Kingdom. I speak as a former pastor, knowing my own experience and being acquainted with many others in pastoral ministry.

We tend to be too satisfied with *"affecting only a restricted part of the organism"* of the Kingdom of God. So much of our local church structure in our culture is geared to the strength and security of the people who are involved in the particular local church, basically the leadership and their followers. As leaders, we often want to bring them in and keep them in. We want to count "nickels and noses" to quote a speaker I recently heard. We focus on the sheepfold much more than the harvest field.

Part of the reason for this is that almost all church leaders are called "pastors," even if their gifting is one of the other ministries. We have senior pastors, associate pastors, youth pastors, children's pastors, senior's pastors, single's pastors and a few other types of pastors. Those who fill these rolls feel the expectations of people to "pastor" their group.

Many of them actually need to be freed up to be apostles, prophets, evangelists and teachers. True pastors are very important and necessary, with the majority of them being incredibly hard workers and having great hearts for the flock, but they can't do it all. And they can't do a really great job of something God never called them to do.

Apostles will proclaim the "Kingdom" mandate to bring the Kingdom to the King and cast vision for accomplishing greater things for God. Prophets will stir up the spirit of the warriors and shake up those who are "at ease in Zion." Evangelists will carry the gospel to the ends of the earth, and the teachers will bring appropriate levels of revelation to the babes and also to those who are more mature.

The dominant "pastoral" control of the direction and focus of the church does not emphasize the Kingdom; it emphasizes the "local" church, its people and leadership. Finances are directed to the needs of the flock and the shepherds, while very little in comparison goes to outreach and harvest.

The gospel is spreading in Africa, especially in places like Mozambique, Uganda and Nigeria, because most of the focus is on the Kingdom and the task of going and getting the Bride of Jesus Christ, rather than managing and growing the local church. Thousands of new churches have sprung up, but every church leader is made to be so aware of the heart of Jesus for the lost. Those called "pastors" are also released to be evangelists who take in orphans and spread the gospel throughout their villages and surrounding communities. Many are more apostolic in gifting and plant numerous churches and help train leaders.

Rolland and Heidi Baker and other "trailblazers" are shaking up the western church whenever they minister in churches and conferences here. Western leaders are made to wonder what is going on when so much is being accomplished by so few who are using such unsophisticated methods and styles of ministry.

Our professionalism and pursuit of excellence (which is a good thing) is being overshadowed and outdone by those without education and sophistication, who function mostly on passion, simplicity and love for Jesus and the lost. I, myself, have been radically renewed in my mind, just observing them, and have now powerfully witnessed what I have preached about for so many years—the restoration of the book of Acts in our day.

The expression "local church" was of course never used in the Bible. There was the church of Ephesus, Corinth, etc., and the "church that is in your house," but they didn't use the limiting word "local." The church of the city would work as one unit, interacting with the apostles, prophets and teachers who would come and go, but a portion of the church of the city could meet in a house and still be "the church."

The word, "church" means "called out." Unfortunately, too many times our main focus is on calling people "in." We want them "in" our "local" church. And of course, they need to be part of a church and nourished into some level of maturity. But God is calling many young and old Christians "out" of the safe, the secure and the comfortable and into the more unpredictable, un-safe harvest fields of the world. It takes work, sacrifice and it requires taking a risk. Protection is needed for newborn babies, but young men and women want adventure and challenge. Un-fortunately, many weary and burned-out leaders are at the stage where they desire peace and security for themselves, more than they want to lead their people on risky adventures into uncharted territory.

But make no mistake about it—going after the harvest is the most thrilling and fulfilling thing we could ever do. Just ask any of the team members that journeyed with us to Mozambique, who saw the miracles and the hundreds of Muslim hands that were raised to accept Jesus at every single outreach. Ask a young lady named Liz. Ask her parents or her sister, Sarah. Ask the older missionaries who didn't formerly believe in the supernatural power of God. Ask the almost two hundred "Holy Given" mission stu-dents on the field, who flocked to Mozambique to learn from Rolland and Heidi Baker, their associate, Lesley-Anne Leighton, and numerous other outstanding contemporary Christian trail-blazers.

So how do we apply this? As leaders we need to search our hearts and motives. How passionate are we about the harvest? Are we and others encouraged and activated to do the work of an evan-gelist? Are we "Kingdom" leaders or just "local" church builders?

When we build the "local" church, and achieve some level of "success" in doing so, there is a lot of personal blessing that comes to us as pastors in the area of prestige, financial security and influence. That can be a reward for faithful and difficult work, but it can also be a subtle and wrong motive for that success. When we simply focus on building the Kingdom however, we often have to lay those things down. We may have to "lose" our life before we "find" it.

We found the above to be true when we made commitments to overseas trips without the finances. We almost came home to financial disaster, but God had put faith in our hearts to believe for miracles, and He came through for us and we didn't have to tell anyone our needs.

Recently I visited a church where I was not speaking, and I heard numerous complimentary references to the local church and the denomination. But there was no mention of supporting other churches or denominations or working in harmony for the harvest and the Kingdom. In the same community, a local church had a sign which read, "We don't put on a show; we preach the Bible." This was clearly a dig against a newer church in the community which was growing rapidly, and clearly revealed a spirit of competition.

And I find that is all too typical. We want to be right and we want to be successful. It produces the "local church" and "our denomination" or "our movement" mentality that pervades the western church. We want to build what will make us look and feel successful. It is such a subtle and pervasive drive within us. Again, I speak from experience, not to judge or criticize, but to motivate you as I have been motivated by others.

It would be helpful to change much of our terminology that boxes us into the old mold and compares us to other churches and movements, as if we are in competition with them. The expression "our church" may be a dead giveaway of our concepts. We may be running the risk of having taken ownership of what belongs only to God.

Perhaps the term "mobile church" would convey a better concept. We want to be known as people who are the church wherever the church is needed. When we think of "church," we should not be thinking of a building or anything that boxes us in. We should be thinking of God's people out in the community, serving Him in every part of society and coming together frequently to exchange "war stories" and encourage one another.

Jesus told us to go into the world and make disciples, and said, "I will build MY church." Let's go out of the box and into the harvest. Let's make disciples of Jesus and not of ourselves. Let's help Him build His church and be His stewards of His church but not the owners. Let's fulfill our apostolic call if we have received one and not be held back by a label that doesn't really fit us.

Let's rethink our financial budget and focus more on "out there" and less on "in here." Let's empower the younger people who possess the zeal and energy and send them to places where God is moving, without fear that we will lose control of them or that they will join another church or movement. Fear of loss is a terrible chain around many leaders' necks. That chain is a very useful tool for our enemy to keep people from fulfilling their destiny. I don't want to criticize the church, but I have seen it too often.

The best way to restructure our churches is to ensure that apostles and prophets and evangelists are released into leadership, along with the pastors and teachers, and given freedom to function in their giftings. They should be chosen not based on their personal proclamations of who they are, but based on humble service to the body through their respective giftings. Apostles and prophets, being foundation stones in the house of God will see the bigger picture and, along with the evangelists, they will care more about Kingdom issues than internal ministry.

Confidentially, pastors, we are discovering very quickly that there is a whole generation of young people, as well as folk of all ages, that are really tired of "church" as we have traditionally known it. They love Jesus, but want to be led into something more challenging than sermons on how to fix their problems. They want to be equipped to impact and change the world. God put that desire in them. If we say, "They'll mature eventually and become less idealistic and more realistic and find their place in the local church," we will have really missed our opportunity to mobilize God's army to win the world for Christ.

Of course they won't be mature at the beginning. And they will have character defects. But we don't have to give them titles or positions. They don't need to be deacons or elders. We just have to empower them to serve Jesus. God gave me a word of wisdom in Mozambique that goes like this: "The youth of today will be matured and refined in the fires of revival." Preaching guilt and condemnation won't mature them, but letting them partake of true revival will. I experienced it in my own life, and I have seen it in many others, including those who went with us on our recent trip to Mozambique.

I mentioned above the concept of "spreading" the gospel. The thought came to me that we spread peanut butter on our bread, after we extract a clump of it from the jar and place it on the slice of bread. We don't leave it in a lump in the middle. We spread it to every part of the bread. In the west, we often have the gospel in lumps we call churches, but God wants to spread it over the whole city or region or nation.

I don't have all the answers. I don't even know all the questions. But I'm sure we can do better than we are doing now if we get low enough in the presence of Jesus and ask Him what we can change to bring our ministry into conformity with His vision for it.

God never rejects a humble heart, but He has promised to resist the proud. Humility needs to be worked at. Pride doesn't. It comes naturally, even to us in ministry leadership. It has infected us all and keeps coming up like last summer's weeds that you've already pulled over and over again. I have been in pastoral ministry for almost thirty years and I know the battles that I and my fellow-pastors in our communities had to deal with all the time.

Before concluding this chapter, I want to report the exciting news that changes are happening in the western church that are extremely encouraging. Just in the past few years and especially the last month or so, I have heard of numerous cases of churches doing things that were unheard of in previous decades. Many apostolic "pastors" have led their churches to give large amounts of money to help other churches in their cities. In addition, they have given more of their personal time and resources for missions projects and evangelism, often working sacrificially to help other ministries in their cities to flourish.

Some of the leading examples of a "Kingdom mindset" included Colorado Springs pastor, Ted Haggard, author of "Primary Purpose" and now president of the American Association of Evangelicals. Other wonderful examples include Bill Johnson of Redding California and Ché Ahn of Pasadena, California.

But many others in smaller ministries are also leading by example. Right here in Douglasville, Georgia, a suburb of Atlanta, where we are presently ministering, a young fiery pastor/evangelist, named Vance Murphy, leads a fairly small church that joins forces with another ministry in Kentucky, establishing "Father's House" homes for abandoned children in many nations. In nine months, since we met in Mozambique, he has gone to India, the Ukraine, Brazil and Guatemala, helping abandoned children in these needy nations. In addition, they serve the poor in their city in various outreaches. They are such an example of Kingdom passion and a church that is not just "local," a church that embraces the apostolic, prophetic and evangelistic ministries along with the pastors and teachers.

I know that it seems like finances are not available for such adventures for most church leaders. Even though I loved missions, having journeyed to other nations four times, when we started a new church in a small town, I never left North America for eighteen years. We had a very tight budget and although much of our ministry was reaching out to the lost, we had very little immediate impact on the Kingdom of God at large.

The good news is that today, there is a major shift in Kingdom financing. And I believe that every church leader who catches the vision and feels the passion for the great Kingdom harvest, which is now in full swing, will see miraculous provision to finance those who want to be a part of the harvest. God is moving in powerful ways among the youth, as we so clearly witness in meetings from city to city. The older generation is becoming more challenged to help finance the younger generation, and there is a tremendous increase in short term mission trips by both younger and older Christians.

God is also raising up many "Market Place Apostles," who are being used to generate large amounts of money to support worldwide evangelism. Exciting new technologies and business opportunities are being released from Heaven at this writing to empower the harvesters. God knows how ripe the harvest is, and He is not willing to let it be lost for lack of finances.

Let's get excited, renew our minds, shift our priorities and participate in the worldwide harvest. Let's spread the gospel, make the whole world our parish and let Jesus build His church.

May those with spiritual ears hear what the Spirit is saying to the churches. Amen!

BEN R. PETERS

With over 35 years of ministry experience, Ben Peters with his wife, Brenda, have been called to an international apostolic ministry of equipping and activating others. As founders and directors of Open Heart Ministries, Ben and Brenda have ministered to tens of thousands with teaching and prophetic ministry. The result is that many have been saved, healed and delivered and activated into powerful ministries of their own.

Ben has been given significant insights for the body of Christ and has written eight books in the past five years, since beginning a full-time itinerant ministry. His passions and insights include unity in the body of Christ, accessing the glory of God, five-fold team ministry and signs and wonders for the world-wide harvest.

The Peters not only minister at churches, camps, retreats and conferences, but also host numerous conferences with cutting-edge apostolic and prophetic leaders. They reside now in Northern Illinois with the youngest three of their five children, and travel extensively internationally.

Open Heart Ministries
www.ohmint.org
benrpeters@juno.com
15648 Bombay Blvd.
S. Beloit, IL 61080

Printed in the United States
38778LVS00003B/334-351

9 780976 768555